THE IMAGE OF RIGHTEOUSNESS

YOU'RE MORE THAN YOU KNOW

DR. CREFLO A. DOLLAR JR.

Harrison House
Tulsa, Oklahoma

The Image of Righteousness:
You're More Than You Know
ISBN 1-57794-453-4
Copyright © 2002 by Dr. Creflo A. Dollar Jr.
Creflo Dollar Ministries
P.O. Box 490124
College Park, GA 30349

Published by Harrison House, Inc.
P.O. Box 35035
Tulsa, OK 74153

TABLE OF CONTENTS

PREFACE

For more than eighteen years I have repeatedly studied the subject of righteousness, and I am still amazed by it. Each time I thought I fully understood righteousness I would uncover deeper layers of revelation knowledge, which forced me to admit I had much more to learn.

It is much deeper than we think.

Our righteousness in Christ is the centerpiece on which Christian faith is built. Everything God's Word promises us hangs on it, and the entire structure of our salvation is built upon it. If we are going to walk in the joy of our salvation and the power of the promises we have in Him, we *must* understand our righteousness in Christ.

When Christians hear the word *righteous,* nearly all of us think we understand what it means. The biggest part of the problem is that *very few* understand. We only *think* we do. Often, our religious traditions have distorted our understanding of righteousness. Consequently, the authority that God intended for us to have has been rendered totally ineffective.

This means some of our religious traditions have to die. That's okay. The truth is, many of us have been at the mercy of inaccurate scriptural translations injected with personal theologies. We've been victims of a "Well, that's the way we've always done it" kind of thinking. The watered-down traditions that have resulted have seduced many into a powerless, ineffective form of religious thinking instead of the vital, dynamic faith that really can move mountains.

Think about it. If traditions and religious thinking have all the answers, then why are so many of us living broke, disgusted, and defeated lives? Why are our kids still plagued with drugs? Why are debts still overwhelming to so many of us? Why are so many people still dying of cancer?

The raw truth, for so many people, is that *nothing* is working. Why? Because something is missing. A major part of the equation is simply not there; that is, a proper understanding of our righteousness in Christ.

This book was written to help God's righteousness become real in your life. In fact, I want it to be so real that Satan loses his grip on you. I want you to experience the life and power God intends for you to have through the gift of righteousness. If you attain an unshakable confidence in the righteousness of God, then *The Image of Righteousness* will have achieved its purpose and the righteousness of God will make a mark in your life that cannot be erased!

THE MASTER KEY

What would you say if I told you there is indeed a master key that unlocks everything in the kingdom of God here on earth? What would you say if I told you that the key is already in your possession? What if I told you that it is God's desire for all of us to have the power to transform our lives and the lives of those around us?

To be used by God in these last days, to accomplish something significant for the kingdom of God, we must discover and learn how to use the master key.

God has not hidden full understanding of this master key from us. In fact, those of us who have accepted Jesus as our Lord and Savior possess this key. God has revealed this master key to us through His Word; when we use the key properly, it will open to us the endless treasure of His grace. When we unlock that treasure, we will finally be able to live in the blessings bought and paid for by the blood of Jesus.

1

I want to warn you, though, that when you hear the truth concerning the master key, you will be tempted to think, *Oh, I know what that is,* or, *I understand that concept.* The reality is that many of us do *not* understand it; we only *think* we do.

I know this because I thought the same thing years ago. Over the last couple of years, however, while searching the Word on a subject totally unrelated, new revelation proved how shallow my understanding was. I realized that I would have to hit the books again and that some of my long-held religious beliefs would have to change. I had to do this because religious traditions have robbed many of us of the deep and rich relationship God desires to have with us.

I am convinced that man-made doctrines of religious tradition are the greatest enemy of the church today. This kind of religion creates a consciousness and a system of beliefs that can cause us to completely misunderstand our relationship with God. This form of religion denies the life and power of the gospel of Jesus.

Now, after eighteen years of periodic study and three years of intense study, I share this master key with you. It will be no surprise to me, however, if the Lord is not yet finished revealing layers of understanding concerning this subject.

Righteousness is the master key. By correctly understanding how righteousness works in God's plan for man, we can more effectively use this master key to open the treasures of the kingdom of God.

JUSTIFIED BY RIGHTEOUSNESS

Let's begin with a foundational Scripture that puts the various elements of righteousness in perspective. Let's examine this passage from Romans chapter 3 in *The Amplified Bible*. It is a bit long, but I encourage you to slowly read it all the way through.

For no person will be justified (made righteous, acquitted, and judged acceptable) in His sight by observing the works prescribed by the Law. For [the real function of] the Law is to make men recognize and be conscious of sin [not mere perception, but an acquaintance with sin which works toward repentance, faith, and holy character].

But now the righteousness of God has been revealed independently and altogether apart from the Law, although actually it is attested by the Law and the Prophets,

Namely, the righteousness of God which comes by believing with personal trust and confident reliance on Jesus Christ (the Messiah). [And it is meant] for all who believe. For there is no distinction,

Since all have sinned and are falling short of the honor and glory which God bestows and receives.

[All] are justified and made upright and in right standing with God, freely and gratuitously by His grace (His unmerited favor and mercy), through the redemption which is [provided] in Christ Jesus,

Whom God put forward [before the eyes of all] as a mercy seat and propitiation by His blood [the cleansing and life-giving sacrifice of atonement and reconciliation, to be received] through faith. This was to show God's righteousness, because in His divine forbearance He had passed over and ignored former sins without punishment.

It was to demonstrate and prove at the present time (in the now season) that He Himself is righteous and that He justifies and accepts as righteous him who has [true] faith in Jesus (Rom. 3:20-26 AMP.)

Notice what's at stake where our righteousness is concerned: justification. We are either justified by faith or not at all.

"Therefore by the deeds of the law there shall no flesh be justified..." (v. 20). That word *justified* means "declared righteous."[1] In other words, we are righteous for no other reason than the fact that God has declared us righteous.

Verses 21-22 say, "...being witnessed by the law and the prophets; even the righteousness of God which is by faith...."

Righteousness by faith is a little like being born into a family. I was born into the Dollar family. I am a Dollar based on my family's declaration. I did not have to do anything to become a part of the Dollar family. My parents simply declared me "Creflo Dollar."

The same kind of dynamic is at work when we are born again. When we realize we need a Savior to forgive our sins and bring us into fellowship with God, and we ask Jesus to do those things, we are born again. When we are born again, we are declared righteous and made members of the family of God. Being born again does not include instructions on how to do something to become righteous. They are not necessary. We are born again and declared righteous by the Word through our faith and belief in Jesus Christ.

JUSTIFIED BY FAITH

Justification by declaration began with Abraham.

What shall we say then that Abraham our father, as pertaining to the flesh, hath found? For if Abraham were justified by works, he hath whereof to glory; but not before God. For what saith the scripture? Abraham believed

Abraham was righteous purely because he *believed* God.

God, and it was counted unto him for righteousness. Now to him that worketh is the reward not reckoned of grace, but of debt. But to him that worketh not, but believeth on him that justifieth the ungodly, his faith is counted for righteousness (Romans 4:1-5).

[But] if so, what shall we say about Abraham, our fore-father humanly speaking—[what did he] find out? [How does this affect his position, and what was gained by him?]

For if Abraham was justified (established as just by acquittal from guilt) by good works [that he did, then] he has grounds for boasting. But not before God (Rom 4:1-2 AMP)!

Notice that if Abraham's acquittal, deliverance, and justification had come by good works, then he would have had the right to boast. However, the Scripture says, "Abraham believed in (trusted in) God, and it was credited to his account as righteousness (right living and right standing with God)" (Rom. 4:3 AMP).

Abraham was righteous purely because he *believed* God.

The righteousness Abraham received is the righteousness provided to him by the covenant God made with him. A covenant can be defined as "an agreement between two or more parties to carry out the terms agreed upon" or "a blood-sworn oath that can only be broken by death." Out of that covenant, righteousness was born.

After these things the word of the Lord came unto Abram in a vision, saying, Fear not, Abram: I am thy shield, and thy exceeding great reward.

And Abram said, Lord God, what wilt thou give me, seeing I go childless, and the steward of my house is this Eliezer of Damascus? And Abram said, Behold, to me thou hast given no seed: and, lo, one born in my house is mine heir.

And, behold, the word of the Lord came unto him, saying, This shall not be thine heir; but he that shall come forth out of thine own bowels shall be thine heir. And he brought him forth abroad, and said, Look now toward heaven, and tell the stars, if thou be able to number them: and he said unto him, So shall thy seed be (Gen. 15:1-5).

Out of God's covenant with Abraham, the everlasting, unconditional love of God was manifested toward all who believe.

Out of God's covenant with Abraham, the everlasting, unconditional love of God was manifested toward all who believe.

What did Abraham do to deserve God's visitation and offer to enter into covenant with Him? Nothing. No righteous deeds, no salvation prayer. Yet, God showed up one day to make Abraham a promise. He promised Abraham that He would make him a

6

father of many nations, that He would prosper and bless him; and Abraham agreed.

God was looking for someone who would simply believe Him so He could manifest His goodness toward Abraham and generations to follow. He could not bless Abraham if he would not believe Him.

Let's say for instance that I am a stranger. If I ask you to meet me so that I can give you $10,000, and you don't believe me, you probably will not agree to meet me. Maybe you're thinking, *I don't know you,* or, *I don't deserve what you're trying to give me.* In any event, if you don't believe me, I am unable to give you anything.

Years ago, I was shopping at a well-known shoe store and overheard a man who was inquiring about layaway for a pair of shoes he had selected. The Lord spoke to me and said, *Buy those shoes for him.* So, I approached the man and asked if those were the shoes he wanted. They were, he replied. I then asked the clerk to wrap them up and give the man his shoes and I would pay for them. However, the man was unable to receive the gift because he couldn't believe that a stranger would actually buy him a pair of shoes. He felt that he had to do something in return for what I had offered.

Sadly, he felt he had to earn the gift. He had a problem with receiving. As a result, I could not give it to him even though I really wanted to.

All God wanted Abraham to do was believe Him. Abraham would have never known about God's love or His giving without first believing Him. Neither would he have known about His power or His righteousness without first believing.

I believe God's plan for man is simple. Yet, you will never experience any of God's promises until you do what Abraham did—believe: "And he believed in the Lord; and he [God] counted it to him for righteousness" (v. 6).

The Bible says that Abraham was a righteous man because he believed what God said.

From then on, whatever else God said, he also believed—even when it came to his son.

You will never experience any of God's promises until you do what Abraham did—believe.

And he [God] said, Take now thy son, thine only son Isaac, whom thou lovest, and get thee into the land of Moriah; and offer him there for a burnt offering upon one of the mountains which I will tell thee of (Gen. 22:2).

Why would God tell a man to take his own son, whom he loved, and kill him? Abraham needed Isaac because there was no way his seed could continue unless Isaac was preserved.

If Abraham was going to have offspring that would outnumber the stars according to the promise of Genesis 15:5, then Isaac had to live. Abraham *had* to have believed God, expecting that something would happen to preserve his son. By believing God, Abraham was made righteous.

THE ACTION OF FAITH

We often hear people say that they believe. Yet, until we understand the connection between belief and faith, we will wonder why our prayers remain unanswered. If it seems that our prayers are not being answered, God is not to blame. We have to look at ourselves. It may be that we have to learn the connection between belief and faith.

Belief can refer to the mental acceptance of something as truth, though absolute certainty may be absent. A problem arises, however, when you believe something to be true and never act on it. This is where faith comes in.

Faith is *acting* on what you believe. It is the appropriate, corresponding, suitable, and proper action. For example, when you sit in a chair, you believe that the chair will provide support. Therefore, the appropriate corresponding action is to sit in the chair—with no thought concerning the chair's ability to support you.

For years we have declared that we were standing in faith for our healing when, in fact, we have only *believed* in God's ability to heal. We have also confessed God's delight in the prosperity of his servant, yet we have never moved from that place of belief.

Faith requires *corresponding* action, not just any action. (James 2:17,20,26.) For example, if someone believes that God is going to heal his or her eyes, there has to be some kind of action; otherwise, it is not faith.

We have to find an action that will correspond with the release of our faith. However, many of us have acted improperly by doing things that did not correspond with our faith. In the case of believing for restored eyesight, for example, some of us have stopped wearing our glasses. Well, that is not going to work if we cannot see without them. Many of us have judged our faith on the action part when it was the wrong action.

In a situation like this, you should thankfully declare that your eyes are totally healed and put on your glasses. The *action* of putting on your glasses corresponds with your faith to be healed.

Belief starts everything. Unbelief stops anything. You may say, "I believe," but something else is required.

Exercising your faith is the corresponding action to your belief according to the Word of God. Faith is what carries it to completion. Abraham believed God, and God called it righteousness. Belief got it started. God showed up in Genesis 15 and made a covenant with him. In effect, God said, "I have to persuade him to believe. If I can persuade him to believe, he can begin the process."

In order for Abraham to become the Father of Faith, his action had to correspond with what he said he believed; hence, the trip to Mount Moriah to slay his son. (Gen. 22.)

Many of us have judged our faith on the action part when it was the wrong action.

People often wonder if God will do something for them. Yet, they have never come to the point of completing the necessary requirements to begin the process. They pass off wishing as believing. There is absolutely no faith in wishing. In and of itself, believing will not bring anything to pass; neither will wishing. At some point you have to believe what the Word of God says and begin to move forward with a corresponding action.

Are you still believing God for something and frustrated because you have not seen it? Then come out of belief mode, and get into action mode. When you believe it so much that you are willing to say it and act on it, your faith becomes ignited. You can then expect God to do great things.

The test of belief is the movement it produces.

The test of belief is the movement it produces. The centurion's belief that Jesus could heal his servant moved him into the presence of Jesus. When Jesus heard the centurion say, "Speak the word only and my servant shall be healed," He also heard great faith for healing. Then the man's servant was healed. (Matthew 8:5-10.)

When the angel Gabriel declared that Mary would have a son named Jesus, she chose to believe him. Her corresponding action was her statement, "Be it unto me according to thy word" (Luke 1:38).

If you believe you are the righteousness of God, it will move you to begin exercising your rights. If you believe God can remove your debt, you will begin to apply the principles that will release you from debt. If you believe God can heal your body, you will activate the principles that will bring healing.

Say this out loud with all your heart:

Heavenly Father, I declare now that my beliefs shall not stand alone. Your Word declares that I have been given the measure of faith, so right now I add that measure of faith to my beliefs. By faith I declare that I am justified. I am the righteousness of God by faith. I live by faith.

Father, I believe; therefore, I will exercise my rights. Lord, my belief moves me, and my faith has appeared. I walk by faith and not by sight. I walk by the Word of God. This is my faith and I receive it now, in Jesus' name!

Doubt and unbelief, go! Leave me now, for I live by faith. Amen.

THE FREE
GIFT

CHAPTER TWO

Even the righteousness of God which is by faith of
Jesus Christ unto all and upon all them that believe: for
there is no difference (Rom. 3:22).

Righteousness is available to all Christians and non-Christians
alike. Though non-Christians may not choose to walk in righteousness, it *is* available to them. Righteousness is available to
every man, woman, and child.

While Romans 3:22 says righteousness is available to everyone, only those who believe the declaration of faith in Jesus Christ
actually become righteous.

Here's an illustration. When you sin, what do you do to make
it right with God? You go to Him and repent based on 1 John 1:9,

which says that if we confess our sins, He is faithful and just to forgive our sins and to cleanse us from all unrighteousness.

How do you know that you received forgiveness when you confessed your sins to God? You cannot feel anything. You simply believe that you've received your forgiveness.

Many people think they have to do something more than simply act on what the Word says in order to be forgiven. They don't really believe that forgiveness is as simple as confessing your sins and relying on God's willingness to forgive. They don't believe they can receive their forgiveness and move on without being concerned about it anymore.

Forgiveness is based on God's promise, not human feeling.

Human nature says forgiveness cannot be that easy. Our natural thinking makes it difficult for us to believe that our sins can be erased, allowing us to stand guiltless before God. Human nature says there must be pain and suffering to really be forgiven. Forgiveness is based on God's promise, not human feeling.

In fact, according to Psalm 103:12, when your prayer for forgiveness reaches God, He takes the sin, rips it out of your journal, and throws it as far as the east is from the west. Hebrews 8:12 says that He remembers it no more. If you were to talk to Him about every sin you have ever committed, He would choose to not even acknowledge them. With God, it is truly a case of forgive and forget.

Now, you can choose to continue to suffer, but you are not going to be any more forgiven after you suffer than if you had simply believed in God's forgiveness and acted as if you believed that you were actually forgiven.

This example is important because the way you receive forgiveness is the exact same way you receive your righteousness. You must believe you have received it and act as if it is so.

If you do not receive your forgiveness by faith, the next time you stand before God praying, you might be thinking, *I believe I am forgiven;* but if you still have a guilty conscience, you did not truly receive the promise of forgiveness. If you cannot believe that you are forgiven, then neither will you believe the truth that you are the righteousness of God.

It takes faith to believe the Word. My life of faith consists of three things. The first is what God said in His Word. The second is what I choose to receive from God. Finally, I focus on what I must do to act as if I've received it.

If you struggle with believing what is in the Bible, you are struggling with righteousness, because righteousness says you are right with God even when you have done wrong.

If you struggle with believing what is in the Bible, you are struggling with righteousness.

Righteousness says that even after you curse someone, you are still the righteousness of God. Although you must repent of your sin, your behavior has nothing to do with whether or not God will forgive you.

We must renew our minds to righteousness to truly understand how it can work effectively in our lives. Many of us have been seduced by religion. Throughout our lives, we thought that righteousness was based on all the good things we did. The more good things we did, the more righteous we felt.

The truth is, God made us righteous through the blood of Jesus when we accepted Him as our Savior and Lord. We cannot *make* ourselves righteous through good deeds.

God said, "I will declare as righteous everyone who receives My Son, Jesus, by faith." When you are born again, that declaration becomes active in your life. It's just like when God created the world: His spoken Word brought into reality the very words He spoke. You are righteous because you accepted His free gift of salvation through faith in Jesus. As a result, His declaration of your righteousness became a reality in your life.

SIN CONSCIOUSNESS VS. RIGHTEOUSNESS CONSCIOUSNESS

I must clarify something here. So far, the subject has been the righteousness of God; it has not been sin. However, some of us are more conscious of sin than we are of righteousness. Many preachers have taught for so long that all have sinned and come short of the glory of God. While this is true, Paul is not trying to focus our attention on sin in Romans chapter 3. What he is saying is that righteousness is available to all. However, it is only upon all who believe.

Even the righteousness of God which is by faith of
Jesus Christ [is] unto all and upon all them that believe: for

there is no difference: for all have sinned and come short of the glory of God (Rom. 3:22-23).

All that is needed to be a sinner is to be born. (Ps. 51:5; Rom. 5:12.) Stealing, cursing, and robbing are merely the result of the sin that is our birthright.

Since everyone is born into sin, Paul is saying that God has provided something to counteract our sin; that is, His righteousness. Because all have sinned, *all* can receive the righteousness of God through faith in Jesus.

Sin is our birthright as human beings. We are born into it. However, righteousness is our birthright as Christians. We are born into it through the new birth and no longer have an inheritance of sin.

We know that righteousness is free. We also know that we could not, and did not, earn it.

Righteousness is our birthright as Christians.

We know that God's righteousness comes through a declaration. The effect of that declaration is upon those who believe and receive Jesus by faith as Lord and personal Savior into their lives.

We also know that anyone born a sinner (that means everyone) can receive God's righteousness.

Now read this out loud: *I am the righteousness of God right now. Regardless of my past behavior, regardless of what I may do in the future, my faith in Jesus makes me the righteousness of God.*

AN UNQUESTIONABLE RIGHT

Think about this. What allowed Jesus to walk untouched through a crowd of people who wanted to kill him? How did He cast out the worst diseases ever seen on a physical body, and command healing with fearless confidence? How did He cast the demon out of a person, causing the demon to flee in terror? How did He stand up in a boat and command peace in the midst of a storm?

It's simple. Jesus knew He had an unquestionable right to do these things. There was nothing anyone could say to change His mind.

He *has* that right—and so do you.

The reason so many believers do not operate at the same level of power as Jesus did while on earth is that they do not accept the certainty of faith He has. He not only had the right to perform those miracles, but He could not be persuaded otherwise. When Jesus spoke the Word in fearless confidence, He expected something to happen.

Likewise, when our faith is mixed with fearless confidence in knowing we are the righteousness of God in Christ, we can confront debt and declare it to leave, and then live as though we are free from debt.

People will stand around you wondering why you think things are supposed to happen just the way you say. All you have to do is tell them that you have fearless confidence in knowing that you are the righteousness of God.

Just as Jesus did, we have to know that as sons and daughters of God, we are righteous. Like Jesus, we must have fearless confidence born of absolute faith in the Word of our Father. Believing that it would be as He said it would.

THE ABILITY TO STAND BEFORE GOD

Righteousness is the ability to stand before God without the sense of guilt or inferiority. It is the ability to stand before God and talk to Him as a child to a Father, expecting His response, and knowing that we have a right to receive what we ask because of what He has declared over us.

> **Righteousness is the ability to stand before God without the sense of guilt or inferiority.**

When I am in a very important meeting, only my children can burst into my office and interrupt what I am doing. They are not going to feel guilty at all, because they know they have a right to come to me at any time. They are my children. Their right is born out of our relationship. Without relationship, there is no right. It is the same with the Father and us. Through our relationship with Him, we have rights.

I am righteous; therefore, I can be healed. I am righteous; therefore, I have angelic protection. I am righteous; therefore, I will always triumph in Christ Jesus.

Every promise in the Bible hinges on my acceptance of the righteousness of God. By simply realizing His righteousness in me, the wrong in my life can be fixed. If I am poor, I have a right to prosperity. If I am sick, I have a right to be healed. If I am in bondage, I have a right to be delivered. Everything can be received through God's righteousness in me.

You are as righteous as you are ever going to be. In other words, you cannot become any more righteous than you were the day you accepted Jesus as your Lord and Savior.

Righteousness is not obtained by works. Praying, going to church, tithing, and even walking in love will not make you righteous.

This truth was revealed to me one day as I was going through a process I called "consecration." I locked myself in a room to fast, pray, and seek God. As I was praying, I heard the Lord ask the same question three times: *Son, what are you doing?* Each time my answer was that I was trying to become more righteous. The first two times He responded by saying, *You're already righteous.* I didn't pay attention to Him; I was busy trying to do what I thought would honor my Father. But the third time He answered, I heard something that commanded my attention. He said, *"Son, you are as righteous today as you're ever going to be."* I asked Him what He meant by that. He told me that the day I was born again He made me righteous.

Righteousness is not obtained by works. Praying, going to church, tithing, and even walking in love will not make you righteous. These are things we do because we *are* righteous.

For he hath made him [Jesus] to be sin for us, who knew no sin; that we might be made the righteousness of God in him (2 Cor. 5:21).

When something is created, the end result cannot do anything to help with its creation.

Jesus, who had never sinned, had to be *made* sin in order that we who had been born sinful could be *made* the righteousness of God. A tree does not *try* to be a tree. By nature, it *is* a tree. A man does not *try* to be a man. By nature, he *is* a man. Nothing can change what you are by nature.

Just as nothing can change what we are by nature, sin cannot change our new nature when our nature has been made the righteousness of God.

The battle is not won just because we have received a new nature. Our flesh still wants to return to some of the same sinful things we did prior to our acceptance of Christ. We have to renew our minds to the reality that we are no longer the same people we used to be. We have a new nature. We are now by nature the righteousness of God.

> **A successful life is the fruit of a mind renewed through the Word of God.**

How do you renew your mind? Mind renewal comes through conforming to and thinking in line with the Word of God.

Do not be conformed to this world (this age), [fashioned after and adapted to its external, superficial customs], but be transformed (changed) by the [entire]

renewal of your mind [by its new ideals and its new atti-
tude], so that you may prove [for yourselves] what is the
good and acceptable and perfect will of God, *even* the
thing which is good and acceptable and perfect [in His
sight for you] (Rom. 12:2 AMP).

You renew your mind by learning all the rights you have as a
righteous person. When you learn your rights, you will begin to know
with certainty that you have a right to be delivered from your sins.

People often think that by being born again, a person automatically enters into perfection. The truth is, when you are born again,
you enter into a process of renewing your mind to remove the old
sin nature of your life. It is important to immediately recognize
that by faith you are the righteousness of God.

RULING AND REIGNING IN LIFE

A successful life is the fruit of a mind renewed through the
Word of God. Although you are already righteous, a constant
renewing of your mind ensures your ability to rule and reign in life.

For if by one man's offence death reigned by one;
much more they which receive abundance of grace and of
the gift of righteousness shall reign [rule] in life by one,
Jesus Christ (Rom. 5:17).

In other words, those who receive the gift of righteousness rule
in this life.

When you accept that you are the righteousness of God, you can rule over your circumstances and your environment just as Jesus did. You can declare that you are the righteousness of God and rule in every area of your life.

Believing you are the righteousness of God covers a lot of areas. You can believe you have authority over sin, and the circumstances of your life.

Once when the weatherman announced that a big storm was headed our way, I stepped out on my front porch and declared that I am the righteousness of God. I spoke to the storm and declared that the storm would not touch my house. Because I am the righteousness of God, I have the right to keep my home safe.

You cannot convince me that the economy or my circumstances are going to have a negative impact on me.

When the storm came, trees fell everywhere, but the destruction stopped at my property line. Why? No harm came to my property because I am the righteousness of God. So are you.

You cannot convince me that the economy or my circumstances are going to have a negative impact on me. My attitude is that I am the righteousness of God. The Bible says that I have ruling power in this earth.

The devil does not rule in this earth. The righteousness of God rules in the earth and I am the righteousness of God. I rule over cancer. I rule over debt. I rule over my enemies. Through the Word, I have been given dominion over the earth.

Righteousness means right standing with God. We have heard it before, but now it makes sense. You are right with God. You stand on a solid footing with Him. You have authority, and a right to stand before God and talk to Him just as you would talk to your earthly father. You can expect answers from Him because you are right with Him. Righteousness is the act of being able to go before God and stand in His presence without any sense of guilt, shame, or inferiority.

> **Righteousness is the act of being able to go before God and stand in His presence without any sense of guilt, shame, or inferiority.**

Here is the question I asked before I understood my right-standing before God in His righteousness: *How in the world can I stand before the Almighty, the perfect King of the universe, the Holy God and Creator of everything, without any guilt for all the sinful things I have done?*

My answer was clearly, I do not have any sin.

The blood of Jesus and His righteousness made it possible for God to declare me righteous when I accepted Jesus. I can stand before Him as righteous because *He* says that I am righteous.

Therefore, I do not allow anything else to influence my attitude about my righteousness before the Father.

YOUR DECLARATION OF RIGHTEOUSNESS

Say this out loud: *Heavenly Father, I declare now that I am the righteousness of God, and I rule and reign in life as the righteous-*

ness of God. Victory is mine because I handle things as the right-eousness of God. I break the hold of sin consciousness over my mind, in the name of Jesus; and I ask You, Holy Spirit, to fill me with the righteousness consciousness that I have a right to, not because of who I am but because of what God has said about me. I pray that something eternal will happen on the inside of me. I thank You that a mark will be made in my life and in the lives of others I touch that cannot be erased because I am the righteous-ness of God. I declare this in the mighty name of Jesus. Amen.

Believe me, something has just been released in your life to unleash all that God has in store for you. It could explode at any time. Expect it!

WEARING YOUR ROBE

CHAPTER THREE

We have heard about being righteous in years past and we have shouted and celebrated, but not always according to [correct and vital] knowledge (Rom. 10:2 AMP).

It is vital that our knowledge concerning the Word is correct, or we will respond as we have so many times before. We will simply *think* we know about it, but what we know will not be life-giving.

The word *vital* really means "life-giving".[1] In the past, our knowledge of the Word has not been life-giving because it has not been correct.

The apostle Paul tells us what has happened concerning our righteousness in Christ.

For they being ignorant of God's righteousness, and going about to establish their own righteousness, have not submitted themselves unto the righteousness of God (Rom. 10:3).

In this passage, Paul makes a distinction between the righteousness of God and the righteousness established by men. The apostle's call in the above verse is for us to submit to, or rely upon, the righteousness of God, rather than attempt to establish our worth or relationship with God based on our own standard of righteousness.

What is the difference between the righteousness of God and the righteousness of men? This concept is very important to understand because it is at the heart of understanding what it means to operate in the righteousness of God.

Let's take the example of the first day you received Jesus as Lord of your life. On that day you recognized Him as the only One who could make a difference in your life. You invited Him to come into your life in a very active way, and when you did, He gave you the free gift of righteousness. You became the righteousness of God. You did not deserve it. You did not earn it. All you did to receive His righteousness was declare Him your Savior and your Lord. At that moment, you were born again and you became the righteousness of God. At this point, if you sinned, what type of battle do you think you created?

Sin makes cowards of men. What is a coward? Someone who is afraid to stand up for what he or she has a right to. Your sin has the potential to make you act like a coward. When you sin, you begin to display characteristics that stop you from standing up for your rights as a believer.

Now consider the battle that sin has created. Your reborn spirit has gone to war with your mind, will, and emotions. You may have believed that you were righteous and could do anything as you spoke the Word. Then soon after, you sinned and did not feel righteous anymore.

Your sin brings guilt. Remember that righteousness is standing before God without a sense of guilt or inferiority. We often wrongly conclude that if we feel guilty, we are no longer in right-standing with God.

Our feelings cannot change the fundamental reality of our righteousness in Christ. We only think they can because we feel badly when we sin.

The voice of the Holy Spirit calls to you, telling you to come back to the spirit of your righteousness and be cleansed from that sin.

> Our feelings cannot change the fundamental reality of our righteousness in Christ.

While the Holy Spirit is speaking to you, your adversary Satan, the accuser of the brethren, works hard to make you feel that there is no way you can be righteous. (Rev. 12:10.) *"Don't you feel guilty?"* he says. *"You knew this born-again thing was too good to be true, didn't you? How could God possibly make you righteous?"*

If we confess our sins, he is faithful and just to forgive us our sins, and to cleanse us from all unrighteousness (1 John 1:9).

When we confess our sins, we are forgiven just as we were on the very first day we believed. As you exercise your right to forgiveness, you maintain your right standing with God. Sin doesn't stop God from seeing you as righteous. Receiving simply allows him to wipe the slate clean, thereby cleansing us from the effects of sin.

It is important to realize that as long as the devil can lead us around by our feelings, he can deceive us into believing his lies rather than what the Word says.

We often try to regain our sense of righteousness to overcome the sense of guilt. We begin to work on our own, setting up new criteria to determine the righteousness of God. Without fail, we end up concluding that if we are going to be truly righteous, we must be perfect and flawless. We conclude that if we aren't, we are not the righteousness of God.

This is what it means to establish our own righteousness. What was originally given as a free gift, we now feel we must maintain through our own standards of self-righteousness. God's explanation of His gift of righteousness is that we are righteous as long as we believe Jesus Christ is our Savior. One of the rights we acquire when we become saved is the right to ask God to forgive us of whatever we have done wrong.

The apostle Paul asked a key question when he wrote to the church at Galatia: "Are ye so foolish? having begun in the Spirit, are ye now made perfect by the flesh?" (Gal. 3:3).

Considering human nature, Paul's question is understandable. On the one hand, we want to believe the Word, which says that we are justified by our faith in Jesus Christ. (Rom. 5:1.) But on the other hand, guilt makes us feel like we don't have a right to communicate with God or fellowship with other believers. Guilt makes us feel disqualified.

Guilt tries to convince us that we cannot be the righteousness of God because of the sins we have committed. Because of this, many people give up because they do not "feel" righteous, even calling themselves sinners.

God qualified you through Jesus to be what the accuser of the brethren says you can never be.

As a result, there are thousands of dear people in the Body of Christ who are afraid to exercise their right to come before God. Instead, they keep score and focus on their sin nature. They continue to remind themselves of their own sin. Then, to make themselves feel better, they remind others of their sin. This tragic mind-set exists even in the church when preachers insist on preaching about sin without reminding people of the righteousness of God.

Listening to people preach about sin will not cause you to walk in righteousness. You are going to continue to make mistakes and wrong choices because you are human. After a while you are going to wonder why you continue coming to church if you cannot meet the standards of man-made righteousness imposed upon you. What has been happening in the Body of Christ is a pattern of setting ourselves up for what is called "our besetting sins." (Heb. 12:1.) These are nothing more than the sins that have not been submitted to the righteousness of God. Many people have tried to defeat them in their own righteousness and have failed repeatedly.

God already knew you could not qualify for His righteousness based on your achievements. That is why He became your Qualifier. God qualified you through Jesus to be what the accuser of the brethren says you can never be.

Your submission to righteousness allows you to follow Jesus' example and expect to be anointed as He is.

Sadly, too many believers spend their lives thinking they have to qualify to be righteous. I carried condemnation and guilt for years as a preacher, thinking I did not have a right to be anointed because I was not righteous enough. I figured other preachers must have been more righteous than I was because of all the miracles performed in their ministries.

I thought, *I'd have to pray ten hours a day and fast three or four times a week.*

In fact, my behavior was establishing the criteria I thought would give me the right to be anointed, instead of simply accepting my righteousness and allowing the power of God to flow through me.

I discovered something very simple, yet very important: Since Jesus is already anointed, if I am in Him I am anointed as well. Therefore, when I lay hands on someone, I am an extension of His hands.

Your submission to righteousness allows you to follow Jesus' example and expect to be anointed as He is. It requires your obedience unto righteousness.

Paul says, "For [Israel] being ignorant of God's righteousness, and going about to establish their own righteousness, have not submitted themselves unto the righteousness of God" (Rom. 10:3).

Many of us have a difficult time submitting ourselves to the righteousness of God, because we have been trained to think that God is not going to forgive us.

CAN YOU IMAGINE?

What would happen if a preacher came to church one Sunday morning and announced to the congregation that because of an argument with his wife, he felt unworthy to preach? Some might think that is noble. Well, it might seem noble, but it would be wrong. That preacher is trying to establish his own righteousness. If the preacher refused to preach in an effort to get right with God, the world may applaud his humility, but according to righteousness, he should have preached. Righteousness is not determined by man's standards but by God's standards.

All that preacher would have had to do was ask for forgiveness and it would be done. He would have been able to continue as if the sin had never occurred.

At some point, we have all missed it, but I pray you catch this revelation: Jesus' blood did the job once and for all, and you are free from sin. Because God declared it so, you are the righteousness of God and you have the right to be cleansed.

If I should miss the mark, I am able to exercise the right to be cleansed because I am in Him.

For Christ is the end of the law for righteousness to every one that believeth. For Moses describeth the righteousness which is of the law, That the man which doeth those things shall live by them (Rom. 10:4).

If you establish your own standard of righteousness, you will have to live by it and do so perfectly. Because you judge yourself by your standards, you are also going to judge everyone else that way.

If you establish your own standard of righteousness, you will have to live by it and do so perfectly.

If you are righteous because of what you do, then in effect, God owes you righteousness as compensation for your good works. God's righteousness would no longer be a gift because you would have *worked* to achieve it. That is not God's plan for righteousness.

Now to him that worketh is the reward not reckoned of grace, but of debt.

But to him that worketh not, but believeth on him that justifieth the ungodly, his faith is counted for righteousness (Romans 4:4-5).

We do righteous things because we are righteous, not because we are unrighteous and have to earn it. We do not pray to become righteous; righteous people pray. We do not go to church to become righteous; righteous people go to church. We do not tithe to become righteous; righteous people tithe. We do not walk in love to become righteous; righteous people walk in love.

I have to believe I am the righteousness of God by faith even when I mess up. Even when I sin and miss the mark, I am still the righteousness of God in Christ by faith.

TRUE HOLINESS

You will never know what true holiness is until you have come to the point of fully accepting your righteousness by faith. For years *holiness* has been defined as "conduct," when in my opinion, holiness should be defined as being of the same mind as God. What He says is good is good in our eyes also; what He says is evil is also evil to us. You are one in mind and heart with God. That is true holiness.

Good conduct is a demonstration of righteousness; it is not what determines righteousness. Much confusion has come about as a result of this misunderstanding. Look again at the verse people frequently quote to support the idea that our conduct determines our righteousness.

> Good conduct is a demonstration of righteousness; it is not what determines righteousness.

If we confess our sins, he is faithful and just to forgive us our sins, and to cleanse us from all unrighteousness (1 John 1:9).

At first glance, this verse seems to be saying that our sins have made us unrighteous; therefore, we have to be made righteous again by confessing our sins. Then God can cleanse us from our unrighteousness.

However, that's not what this verse is saying. If it were, Jesus' dying to purchase our redemption would have been unnecessary. A simple confession of our wrong doing would have made us righteous before the Father.

This verse only pertains to the believer who has been redeemed by Jesus' death on the cross and resurrection. We have been given the robe of righteousness.

I will greatly rejoice in the Lord, my soul shall be joyful in my God; for he hath clothed me with the garments of salvation, he hath covered me with the robe of righteousness, as a bridegroom decketh himself with ornaments, and as a bride adorneth herself with her jewels (Is. 61:10).

We continue to wear our robe of righteousness, but when we sin it is stained. Notice 1 John 1:9 says we are *cleansed,* not redeemed again. If our fundamental righteousness were lost, a simple cleansing would not be enough; we would need redemption again.

However, our right standing with God is based on what Jesus did on the cross. That is far more powerful than any good deed we might do.

We have been made clean through the righteousness of God. We only need to rinse the dust off our feet. (John 13:8-9.) That is the purpose of confessing our sins to the Father. Through our confession, we exercise our right to be cleansed. He has given us the right to be cleansed, and our right standing with Him is not in jeopardy.

That is why we call Him Savior. We have nothing in us that enables us to do this by ourselves. Jesus says, "I was made sin for

you so that you could be made the righteousness of God in Me" (2 Cor. 5:21). The
smart choice is to thankfully and personally
receive what He has done for us.

Righteousness has always been God's
idea. Through Abraham, He initiated the
covenant that introduced righteousness to
humankind. In Jesus, God provided the sacrifice that established His righteousness in
us. God alone was the One who sent His
Son to fulfill all righteousness, and He alone maintains His righteousness in us by the Word of His power.

> **Nothing we do is good enough to achieve a righteous standing before God, or to maintain our righteousness on our own.**

Therefore, regardless of how high our standards are, nothing
we do is good enough to achieve a righteous standing before God,
or to maintain our righteousness on our own. God alone does it all.

When we become fully convinced of the power of righteousness, we will develop backbones of steel. We'll stand confident in
who we are even as Satan attempts to convince us otherwise. Yes,
we've all made mistakes and felt unworthy of the Father's forgiveness, however, He isn't concerned with our former state.

Through Jesus, the Father has done a new thing in us. He
clothed us in His righteousness and notified all of heaven and hell
that we belong to Him. He empowered us with His authority to
reign in victory and enjoy the best in life, and the devil *can't* do a
thing about it. It's an honor to wear His robe of righteousness.
Therefore, let's never forget who we are in Him and the power that
we possess. We are truly more than we think!

YOUR TITLE
DEED

CHAPTER FOUR

The centerpiece of everything God has provided in the Bible is the righteousness of God. Everything hinges on receiving righteousness by faith. If righteousness is not received, we can not receive healing or prosperity. In fact, you must come to a real understanding of righteousness by faith before *anything* in God's kingdom will work for you.

> God made him who had no sin to be sin for us, so that
> in him we might become the righteousness of God (2 Cor.
> 5:21 NIV).

You are not a sinner saved by grace. That is not possible. When you accept Jesus as your Savior, you are rescued from sin. Once rescued, you can no longer be a sinner. You become the righteousness of God. He graces you with His willingness to get involved in your life and gives you His righteousness so that you can be like Him.

Most religious-minded people will try to persuade you differently. Religious-thinking people will tell you that you cannot be like Jesus. In response, you have to believe that you are the righteousness of God no matter what anyone tells you. You are righteous by faith, not by works. You are not righteous by the law, but by faith. You are righteous because He said you are.

The life of righteousness is one that must be lived by faith.

If you do not understand and accept who you are, then your faith is of no value to you. Every time you attempt to exercise your faith, you will struggle with your own thinking if you do not believe you are righteous.

This is what Romans 1 says:

> For in the Gospel a righteousness which God ascribes is revealed, both springing from faith and leading to faith [disclosed through the way of faith that arouses to more faith]... (Rom. 1:17 AMP).

Righteousness does not spring from works; it springs from faith. However, it will also lead you to faith. Righteousness is revealed through faith, and as a result, your faith is increased. The rest of Romans 1:17 AMP reads, "As it is written, The man who through faith is just and upright shall live and shall live by faith."

Your whole life is based on faith when you receive the righteousness of God. You live by faith; therefore, if sickness shows up, you stay in faith. If bills arrive, you stay in faith. If a bad report shows up, you stay in faith. When something adverse happens, that is the perfect time for you to open your mouth, declare your righteousness, and exercise your faith.

PLEASING GOD WITH OUR FAITH

Timing is important. You must understand that there is a due season for everything. You will have to wait until your due season arrives. However, if you are willing to wait forever, standing in faith, you will not be waiting very long. Keep your joy, and continue to believe God. Remember: the just shall live by faith.

The just shall live by his faith (Hab. 2:4).

The just shall live by faith (Rom. 1:17).

The just shall live by faith (Gal. 3:11).

The just shall live by faith (Heb. 10:38).

Without faith it is impossible to please God (Heb. 11:6).

Time and again the Scriptures instruct us to live by faith because faith pleases God. Sadly, many Christians are experienced at being religious but do not know how to live by faith. Some people get upset when people preach about faith. Yet the Scripture says that living by faith is how we please God. The life of righteousness is one that must be lived by faith.

Faith is more than simply believing.

Faith and belief are two sides of the same coin. Belief starts things. Faith is what carries them out.

HOPE, BELIEF, AND FAITH

All through the Bible, Jesus asked people, "Do you believe that I can change your situation?" Many responded, "Oh Lord, I believe." When they did, He said, "That's good enough. Let's get started."

You must have a strong belief to begin whatever it is you want to accomplish. When belief moves from the head to the heart, it will move you into action.

> Now faith is the assurance (the confirmation, the title deed) of the things [we] hope for, being the proof of things [we] do not see and the conviction of their reality [faith perceiving as real fact what is not revealed to the senses] (Heb. 11:1 AMP).

Your faith is the proof or the evidence of what you cannot yet see.

Faith is the assurance of the things you hope for. It does not matter what it is you hope for—a car, a house, a happy marriage, a ministry, a loved one to be saved—you have to have faith before you will see anything come to pass. Your faith is the proof or the evidence of what you cannot yet see. For example, the Bible says, "All things were made by him [God]"

(John 1:3). Faith is the substance of those things that have already been made by God.

Several verses in Genesis 1 say the same thing: "And God *said*...." He spoke everything He created into existence.

What was the result of all that God said? When He said it, He saw it. "And God saw every thing that he had made..." (Gen. 1:31). The words God spoke created everything He said.

"All things were made by him [the Word]; and without him [the Word] was not any thing made" (John 1:3). While faith is the substance of things, the Word that came out of the mouth of God is what made everything. So there has to be a connection between the words that came out of His mouth and the faith that is the substance of everything.

The connection is this: The faith that is the substance of all things is the same faith that was in every word God spoke. Those words contained His faith. So when God spoke His Word, faith came out in the form of words and created everything He said. God, the One who created all things (Heb. 3:4), both visible and invisible, created with His words.

We know God created all things by the power of His Word. Faith is His Word. Now we see the connection between faith and the Word of God.

When God spoke His words, they were filled with faith. Considering that faith equals the Word of God, those who have been declared righteous shall live righteously by the Word of God; that is, by faith.

Everything that is not done by the Word of God, or by faith, is sin. (Rom. 14:23.)

Now faith [the Word of God] is the substance of things hoped for, the evidence of things not seen (Heb. 11:1).

Remember that faith is equal to the Word of God.

What this tells us is that faith is not at its highest level until it gets into your heart *and* into your mouth.

A good man out of the good treasure of his heart brings forth good; and an evil man out of the evil treasure of his heart brings forth evil. For out of the abundance of the heart his mouth speaks (Luke 6:45 NKJV).

We are to have the faith that is in our heart coming out of our mouth continually. Mark 11:22-23 NKJV says, "So Jesus answered and said to them, 'Have faith in God. For assuredly, I say to you, whoever says to this mountain, Be removed and be cast into the sea, and does not doubt in his heart, but believes that those things he says will be done, he will have whatever he says.'"

Faith in your heart is activated by what you say. Your words give faith power to bring what you believe for from the spiritual realm into the natural realm. Your faith to see something grow bigger and bigger in your heart until that faith comes out of your mouth and then your words make it reality in your life.

Romans 10:8 NKJV says, "The word is nigh thee, even in thy mouth, and in thy heart: that is, the word of faith which we preach." Faith has to be in your heart *and* your mouth to see results in your life.

Faith is not something I can see; however, when the Word of God and my faith are the same, I have results that I can see. The Word of God, which I can see, becomes the assurance of the things I cannot yet see. The Word of God is the confirmation. It is the title deed to those things I hope for.

As the righteousness of God, we must exercise what I call "light switch faith."

When you turn on a light switch, you expect the lights to immediately come on. You are convinced that is how it is *supposed* to work.

The Word of God, which I can see, becomes the assurance of the things I cannot yet see.

The same is true with living by faith in God's Word. Light-switch faith says, "I believe the Word and that settles it. I expect results when I operate according to the Word."

When this revelation occurred to me, I thought about prayer, laying on of hands, sowing financial seed and calling those things that be not as though they were. Like the light switch, when we activate our faith in these areas, something is *supposed* to happen. We may not see immediate results in the natural, but that doesn't mean change hasn't occurred in the supernatural realm. As believers, we don't base our lives on what we see. We walk by faith, not by sight (2 Cor. 5:7).

Therefore, we don't have to struggle in an attempt to make our faith work when it looks like nothing is working. Living by faith requires that we trust in the Lord regardless of what we experience. Psalm 37:3 in *The Amplified Bible* says that our trust, reliance, and confidence in Him guarantees our provision for whatever we need. Our trust must be based on the fact that He is faithful to keep his promises to us. Knowing this, our life of faith should be effortless.

At this point, you may not have what you hope for, but you have the Word. When you can find the Scripture that covers your situation, you have your title deed.

That is why the Word of God is so important. We, who live by faith, are not first looking for the manifestation of what it is we hope for. We first look for the title deed to obtain it. The Scripture you find becomes the evidence, or the proof, of what you cannot see. Then this Word is your evidence. It is the evidence needed to prove that what you cannot see does exist.

When you have a Scripture to stand on, you must do something with it in order to activate faith because "faith without works is dead" (James 2:20). You must write it down, speak it out loud, and meditate on it. If you don't experience the results you desire, ask God to help you with any unbelief that might be hindering your manifestation. Allow God's Word to become alive inside of you. Then stay in faith until you can trade the Word for whatever it is you desire. The Word is your title deed to the promise, the proof of what you cannot yet see.

When whatever you desire seems as if it will never show up, go and look at the title deed to remind yourself that somewhere, everything you could possibly desire from God is yours.

You do not have to accept no for an answer once you find the title deed. Operate in this world as the righteousness of God. You have the right to rule and reign. Your title deed is what puts pressure on the unseen to deliver what you hope for, as you wait in faith.

RIGHTEOUSNESS SPEAKS

The righteousness of God (remember, that is you) says, "…The Word is nigh thee, even in thy mouth, and in thy heart: that is, the word of faith, which we preach" (Rom. 10:8).

A person who accepts his or her righteousness speaks the Word of God with confidence at all times. This person says, "By His stripes, I am healed. I am absolutely delivered forever and perfected in Him. I walk in the favor of God. I am anointed from the crown of my head to the soles of my feet. When I pray as the righteousness of God, I get answers to my prayers."

You are the righteousness of God. Therefore, you have a right to say and receive whatever it is that is rightfully yours. This righteousness, which is by faith, speaks.

Righteousness is a Person. Jesus was made your righteousness. (1 Cor. 1:30.) When you put on righteousness, you did not put on an idea or a concept; you put on Jesus in the full richness of His power and glory.

God has declared you righteous. Receive it by faith and say "…be it unto me according to your word," as Mary did (Luke 1:38). Don't be like Zacharias, the father of John the Baptist, who, when he was told that his barren wife would have a son, said, "This cannot be so." Because of his unbelief, he was struck dumb until the birth of his son. (Luke 1:18-20.)

47

Righteousness by faith speaks just as Jesus speaks, just as God speaks. To exercise our rights, they must be spoken. We must publish and declare our rights if we are to exercise them.

> **To the same extent that you receive your righteousness in God through Christ Jesus, you will lose your sin consciousness.**

...The word is nigh thee, even in thy mouth, and in thy heart: that is, the word of faith, which we preach; that if thou shalt confess with thy mouth the Lord Jesus, and shalt believe in thine heart that God hath raised him from the dead, thou shalt be saved. For with the heart man believeth unto righteousness... (Rom. 10:8-10).

If people say that they are born again because they believe in their heart that Jesus is Lord, and do not declare their rights, they cannot enjoy the rights guaranteed them as born-again believers.

Salvation does not only mean that you have a new life in Christ. It also means that you have all of the rights and privileges available to those who are born again. Salvation is the right to be delivered; it is the right to preservation; it is the right to healing; it is the right to soundness. It is also your right standing with God.

As a born-again believer you must speak God's Word continually. When you speak faith-filled words, believing in your heart that you are the righteousness of God, you must declare your rights. In doing this, you come into agreement with what God Himself has already said in His Word. That is why it comes to pass.

...In the mouth of two or three witnesses shall every word be established (2 Cor. 13:1).

When you speak what the Word has already said, you become the establishing witness, and God can bring to pass what you have declared.

Romans 10 is not only a chapter about being born again; it is a chapter that shows you the principle of how righteousness operates. With the heart one believes in Jesus and becomes righteous; and with the mouth the believer's confession makes his life one of righteousness. If you are not saying anything, you are not creating anything and you are not enjoying the rights that you as the righteousness of God should be enjoying. Your silence is hindering the manifestation of God's promises in your life.

Does that mean you can do whatever you want to do and still be the righteousness of God? Not exactly. We will deal with sin and temptation a little later, but consider this.

When a person awakens to righteousness and begins to understand it, his struggle with sin lessens. He begins to lose his sin consciousness and becomes more aware of his righteousness (1 Cor. 15:34). He will begin to confess his rights because he realizes his righteousness. The realization of his righteousness and his acting accordingly will pry the death grip of sin off of his heart. He will not sin, because there is no longer the desire to sin.

To the same extent that you receive your righteousness in God through Christ Jesus, you will lose your sin consciousness. This is extremely important because that is what Jesus died to accomplish.

He shed His blood to buy that right on our behalf.

It's important to understand that even though we have the blood-bought right to have our consciences purged from sin, we can experience that reality only if we declare it by faith.

NATURAL REACTION, SUPERNATURAL ESTABLISHMENT

It is time for us to declare the Word as often as it takes in order to see results in our lives.

We declare our rights in the natural world every day. We have rights as citizens established through law that we exercise as a means of social order. That principle in the spiritual realm might sound like this: *I know I have sinned and missed the mark; but 1 John 1:9 says I have a right to forgiveness, so I exercise that right. Father, I confess my sin of* [name it] *and ask You to forgive me, in Jesus' name. Thank You, Father, that You are faithful and just to forgive me. I receive my forgiveness and cleansing and a conscience purged from that sin.*

We participate in the advocate ministry of Jesus through our confession of sin and our profession of faith. I understand that sometimes it will not seem natural; but keep in mind, we are talking about the supernatural.

It is time to become more aggressive than we have ever been in our lives. It is time for us to declare the Word as often as it takes in order to see results in our lives. We are the righteousness of God, and we do not have to receive anything short of God's promises.

RIGHTEOUSNESS BY FAITH

We live by faith. We come into the blessings of God by faith just as the people of Bible times did.

> We are the right-eousness of God, and we do not have to receive anything short of God's promises.

By faith Abel offered unto God a more excellent sacrifice....

By faith Enoch was translated that he should not see death....

By faith Noah, being warned of God of things not seen as yet, moved with fear, prepared an ark to the saving of his house....

By faith Abraham, when he was called to go out into a place which he should after receive for an inheritance, obeyed... (Heb. 11:4,5,7,8).

By faith, they accomplished so much.

Likewise, if you see a promise in God's Word, then you know by faith it is yours. Knowing that you are the righteousness of God gives you the right to confess that you do not have to be sick and die. By faith, you are healed. (1 Peter 2:24.) You do not have to be broke. By faith, wealth and riches are in your house. (Ps. 112:3.) You do not have to be on the bottom of the economic ladder. By faith, you are prosperous in the name of Jesus. (Ps. 35:27.) You do not have to be in debt all your life and then pass it on to your children. By faith, you are delivered out of debt and your needs are met. (Deut. 15:2.) You do not have to live with a family of sinners on their way to hell, because by faith, your whole household shall be saved. (Acts 16:31.)

By faith, this will be the best year of your entire life. (Isa. 58:14.)

Say this out loud: *Lord, I repent for all those times I have not walked in faith.* Now receive His forgiveness.

EXPLODING FAITH

Begin to walk by faith. You do not have to go on a forty-day fast to try to please God. Just live by faith.

You may read this without understanding it immediately. But when the revelation hits you, you will feel as if something just went off on the inside of you.

That is your faith exploding! All of a sudden, things are going to look easier. Jesus said, "My yoke is easy, and my burden is light" (Matt. 11:30). Your struggle is over right now.

If someone asks why you keep reading the Bible and meditating on and confessing the Scriptures, respond by saying, "I am working on something." "The just shall live by faith" (Rom. 1:17).

BREAKING SIN
CONSCIOUSNESS

CHAPTER FIVE

One of the greatest challenges to walking in the righteousness of God is breaking free of your sin consciousness. Let's study some practical ways to abandon sin consciousness and increase righteousness consciousness.

Therefore if any man be in Christ, he is a new creature: old things are passed away; behold, all things are become new. And all things are of God, who hath reconciled us to himself by Jesus Christ, and hath given to us the ministry of reconciliation; to wit, that God was in Christ, reconciling the world unto himself, not imputing their trespasses unto them; and hath committed unto us the word of reconciliation.

Now then we are ambassadors for Christ, as though God did beseech you by us: we pray you in Christ's stead, be ye reconciled to God. For he hath made him to be sin for us, who knew no sin; that we might be made the righteousness of God in him (2 Cor. 5:17-21).

The reality is that once we are born again, we are a new creation. We are a new creation of being that has never existed before. All things are become new. We have been reconciled to God and have become His ambassadors to the world. But, more importantly, we have become the "righteousness of God." (v. 21.)

At some point, this principle must become a living reality on the inside of you. You must come to the point of acceptance, where you believe this beyond a shadow of a doubt.

For those logical thinkers who need to clearly understand the rationality of something before you can believe it, here is the logic of our righteousness directly from the Scriptures.

> For if because of one man's trespass (lapse, offense) death reigned through that one, much more surely will those who receive [God's] overflowing grace (unmerited favor) and the free gift of righteousness [putting them into right standing with Himself] reign as kings in life through the one Man Jesus Christ (the Messiah, the Anointed One) (Rom. 5:17-19 AMP).

Sin entered the world through one man, Adam. His disobedience separated him from God. This separation is known as spiritual death. Every person born into the earth since Adam has been born under sin and death. Just as one man opened the door to sin for all men, Jesus' obedience unto death has given us spiritual life through His blood. One man's obedience opened the door for all of us to have the opportunity to live in covenant with God.

IT'S NOT GOD'S PROBLEM—IT'S OURS

We often blame God for our failure to receive. We say that because we have not experienced healing or prosperity in our lives. Before casting blame, we must consider whether or not we have received what has been promised us in His Word.

> Neither pray I for these alone, but for them also which
> shall believe on me through their word.
>
> I in them, and thou in me, that they may be made perfect
> in one; and that the world may know that thou has sent me,
> and hast loved them, as thou hast loved me (John 17:20,23).

Jesus Himself has declared that we are in Him and He is in us. That means everything made available to Jesus has been made available to us. It is up to us to receive it.

Even though we hear it, read it, and quote it, the reality of these truths must penetrate our hearts before they can begin to affect our lives. Something has to change in our consciousness in order for these truths to come to pass.

First of all, you have to ask yourself whether or not you have received this gift called righteousness. Examine the stance you have before God. Do you pray as someone who believes they are still guilty? Do you stand before God with condemnation and guilt? Do you still question whether He hears and answers your prayer? Or do you have confidence that you can do what the Bible says you can do? Examine your stance before God.

Your answers to these questions should identify whether you have received this free gift of righteousness. Say this out loud, "I am the righteousness of God."

It may be a challenge to speak these words in confidence right away. But remember, Jesus has already taken care of the sin problem so that you could be made righteous. Settle it in your heart that you *are* righteous.

Begin declaring that you are righteous until you are convinced that you are. (Rom. 4:17.)

By receiving your righteousness, you should be moving to a greater level of confidence and acting more like Jesus.

> But it is from Him that you have your life in Christ Jesus, Whom God made our Wisdom from God, [revealed to us a knowledge of the divine plan of salvation previously hidden, manifesting itself as] our Righteousness [thus making us upright and putting us in right standing with God], and our Consecration [making us pure and holy], and our Redemption [providing our ransom from eternal penalty for sin] (1 Cor. 1:30 AMP).

God made Jesus the righteousness of God for *our* benefit. He also made Him Wisdom, Redemption, and Sanctification for *our* benefit.

THE WORD YOU HEAR

Your receptiveness to the Word you hear is always going to be based on your confidence in that Word.

If your confidence has increased based on what you know of the Word, then most likely you have received it. Your new knowledge is not going to only challenge how you behave, it will also challenge how you think.

If someone says that they have received Jesus as their Lord and personal Savior, there will be indicators of that transformation. Likewise, there are legitimate signs that demonstrate one who has received this free gift of righteousness.

> Your receptiveness to the Word you hear is always going to be based on your confidence in that Word.

There should be signs that suggest that we pray in confidence, knowing that our prayers will be answered. There should be signs that demonstrate that we feel confident about going boldly to the throne of God for help in a time of trouble. There should be signs that we are anointed, knowing that when we lay hands on the sick, they will recover. There should be seed sowing and harvest reaping along with greater confidence, knowing that what God has promised will come to pass. This confidence originates from time spent in the Word of God.

WHY DO SOME CHRISTIANS FAIL?

We hear the Word. We get excited about the Word. We even preach the Word to our friends. That Word should increase our confidence and add boldness to what we do for the kingdom of God. This is where many Christians fail. They make a lot of noise but have no results to show for their effort. Talking is not enough. There is something else we must do. "This book of the law shall not depart out of thy mouth; but thou shalt meditate therein day and night..." (Josh. 1:8). When we spend time meditating in something, we become confident in it.

So it is with the righteousness of God. I am convinced that some of us are going to have to spend time in the Word studying the righteousness of God until we become totally confident of its truth.

This is where the real power, the real anointing, comes. The anointing is the power of God on flesh doing supernaturally what the flesh cannot do alone. (Luke 4:18.) The anointing of God will be produced in our lives when we show we have confidence in the Word we have heard.

The anointing of God will be produced in our lives when we show we have confidence in the Word we have heard.

There is a higher level of anointing available to people who have great confidence in what they receive from the Word of God. Spending time in the Word of God will drive out the questions that religion and the world have put into us over the years. The power obtained by confessing the Word every day will bring you to the point where you realize, just as Jesus did, that what you believe for, have faith for, and confess is *supposed* to happen.

Time in the Word will allow you to become skillful in the Word of righteousness. Suddenly, you begin operating under God's power with complete understanding as a normal part of your everyday life. Your expectations will line up with your meditation.

That is when you know you have really received the righteousness of God. Now you have no fear about exercising your righteousness; you are simply operating under the Word. Suddenly you begin to see great results. As a result of your unquestionable belief, all areas of your life will prosper.

God wants you to use the mind He created and gave to you for His purposes. He gave you an imagination so that you can build blueprints for life. He wants you to imagine yourself debt-free, healed, and delivered. If you can dream about it, you can have it. The blueprint is carefully drawn so that you will increase your faith and see it come to pass. For this to happen, your mind must be renewed.

As a result of your unquestionable belief, all areas of your life will prosper.

Renewing your mind spiritually is no different than doing so naturally. Think about the tasks that you perform now because you have the confidence to do them; for example, driving. At one time you did not have confidence in your driving. You had to spend some time reviewing and studying the procedures. You watched someone. Every time you got in the car, you noticed the procedure. You studied it and became convinced that you could drive. Eventually you did.

The same process applies when we get in the Word. We start meditating in it, receiving it, having confidence in it, and then we receive results.

Scripture says that we cannot begin to know what God is ready to give His people. (1 Cor. 2:9.) But this much I do know: He is waiting for someone who has received Him and His righteousness, someone who will leave his or her sin consciousness behind and move in confidence into what His Word promises.

We have to accept the sacrifice Jesus made as effective for our salvation with all its benefits, and God accepts us in Christ as though we had never sinned. That is the deal, and God is ready to do His part. His free gift of righteousness proves that.

The problem is that many of us lack the confidence to accept what Christ has done for us. As believers we must come to the realization that we have complete and total access to the ministry of Jesus, the complete ministry of the Holy Spirit, and all that the Father has is ours.

For years I did not believe that. But I have more confidence now than ever before. Now that I better understand my righteousness, I understand the whole purpose for a Savior. Now I have complete confidence in my access to the ministry of Jesus. I have access to wisdom. I have access to healing. I have access to the ministry of the Holy Spirit.

As an heir, I have free access to operate in the same anointing as Jesus.

I have access to everything the Father made available to Jesus because I am a son, adopted into the family of God. (John 1:12.) As an heir, I have free access to operate in the same anointing as Jesus. However, I cannot stop there.

I must continue to build on that confidence until it becomes the normal way I live my life. This process destroys the sin consciousness and develops the righteousness consciousness.

The battle from this point on is sin consciousness versus righteousness consciousness. Victory depends on which dominates your thinking.

If sin dominates your thinking, then you are never going to confidently exercise the rights you have through the righteousness of God.

If righteousness dominates your thinking, then you will more easily do the works Jesus did and greater works as well. (John 14:12.) You will also begin to move into the liberty granted you through the righteousness of God.

You need to realize that you have been created in His image; that you are an heir of God and a joint-heir with Christ Jesus; and that you are a son of God. Then you will come to the place where laying hands on the sick will not be a problem. Only then will your consciousness be trained to discern the difference between good and evil.

Now is the time to see results.

It is time for some radically saved people to really believe that they have authority over anything that stands in their way.

When you understand who you are in Christ, demons will tremble. When you walk in righteousness, you look just like Jesus in their eyes.

Up until now we have relied on the authority that comes from a title to produce the power of God in our lives. We have expected the devil and everybody else to roll over because we've called ourselves "Christian" or "Pastor" or "Evangelist."

Corporate executives know that it is ineffective to base authority on job title alone. The title is temporary. When the title disappears, so does the authority.

With the authority of God, the devils can give you any title they want as long as they move when you tell them to move.

THE TITLE OR THE ANOINTING?

Years ago, I considered myself a pastor and teacher and nothing else. At that time, many preachers were calling themselves "Most Honorable," "Bishop," or "Apostle" and adding lots of letters to the ends of their names. The whole thing seemed like a show and it bothered me, so I decided that I would only be called a pastor or teacher.

Feeling that I was being humble and pleasing to the Father, God asked me a question: *Which would you prefer, the title or the anointing?*

Of course, I told Him that I preferred the anointing.

He said, *Then let Me determine the title you will have. Let Me determine who you are going to be, because I might want you to have the anointing of an evangelist one night and because you are stuck on being a teacher, you will not receive it. Or I might want you to be a prophet one night, but if you are so stuck on being the pastor, you will not flow with the anointing. So let Me determine who you are going to be, rather than placing a title on yourself to determine who you are.*

I understood immediately.

Titles don't mean a thing. As children of God, we are full of authority, but that authority has to be exercised. It has to be practiced. Perhaps the first time you lay hands on someone nothing will happen, but you cannot give up. One day your faith and your confessions will collide and a miracle will happen. It only takes one time for that to happen and, believe me, your confidence will increase.

I will always remember when I began miracle services on Saturday mornings. I asked God what would happen if no miracles occurred. I never heard an answer.

One Saturday it seemed as if that was exactly what was going to happen. I kept thinking, *It's hard to believe nothing is going to happen.* In the midst of what I thought was a dry, empty moment, my confidence brought forth a revelation. My confidence said, *What has God already done? Take the number of those you have witnessed as healed and delivered. Let that affect the authority you now possess.* In that instant, I began to minister with a whole new level of confidence.

Several years ago, in Chicago, I laid hands on a young lady. She was in a wheelchair, and her limbs were curled. While there were no visible signs, I knew in my heart she was healed.

I asked her if she believed she was healed. She said yes. So I told her to never let go of her belief.

A year later, she came to visit and sat over in a corner of the church. At one point, she approached me and asked if I remembered her.

She reminded me of who she was and told me that although nothing visible happened when I prayed for her that night, she held onto her belief for healing. After about a month, her body started straightening out and she was healed. I asked her what she was currently doing, and she told me that she was on tour around the country with a choir and doing the will of God.

Her healing began the night we prayed. Neither of us were moved by what we saw during that prayer. It was our trust in the anointing of our righteousness that produced results.

The Word of God works!

THE ESSENTIAL TRUTHS

Do not be moved by what you see or hear. Be moved only by these truths: You are the righteousness of God; you have the authority of Jesus; you have the authority to use His name. As a believer, when you do things according to the Word and according to your rights, things happen.

> For the law having a shadow of good things to come, and not the very image of the things, can never with those sacrifices which they offered year by year continually make the comers thereunto perfect. For then would they not have ceased to be offered? because that the worship-

pers once purged should have had no more conscience [consciousness] of sins (Heb. 10:1-2).

I remember when I first became born again. I also remember the times when I sinned and felt condemned. I developed a sin consciousness that told me I was just a sinner saved by grace. Even preachers would say that as a Christian, I was nothing but a sinner.

I believed them. At that time, I did not expect God to show up in my prayer time. I felt that either I was not worthy or that God was too busy to answer me. Each time I would pray, I would repent of my sins, whether I had sinned or not. I did this out of habit because I was trained to be sin conscious. Of course, nothing was working in my spiritual life and I was moving in a very low level of the anointing.

You do not let your own children speak to you as if they are unworthy to eat your food or wear the clothes you buy for them.

Yet how many Christians have spent years thinking they are unworthy, and have more confidence in going to hell than in going to heaven? How many years have we spent exalting Satan's power above God's power—even after being born again?

Throughout the Bible, you will find Scriptures that say God always causes us to triumph, and we are made new creatures, a new creation of being that have never existed before, and we have wronged no one. (2 Cor. 2:14; 5:17; 7:2.)

However, because of sin consciousness, it is easy to have more confidence in the old sin nature than in the righteousness of God. There was even a time in my own life where I had more confidence in myself than in the power of God's anointing. That had to change.

I have seen that kind of thinking defeat people. I have seen believers who, because of their well-developed sin consciousness, went back to the world. I have known people who thought God hated them because they were unable to live a perfect life.

One day I realized that no matter what I had done, the blood of Jesus is strong enough to deal with my sin, and strong enough to maintain the righteousness of God in my life.

I realized God loved me so much that He sent Jesus so that I would never have to do anything by myself. Now nothing is impossible to me and I can conquer anything that life throws at me. The same is true for you.

In the natural, when you stumble to the ground, you don't sit there complaining about having fallen. You stand to your feet, dust yourself off, and go on about your business.

Likewise, be free from the "I've fallen and I can't get up" mentality where sin is concerned. When you fall into sin, there is no reason to wallow in self-pity for what you've done. Get up in the name of Jesus and stand in your righteousness. Don't beat yourself up. Remind yourself that you're the righteousness of God and repent *immediately*. The more you delay, the more you give place to the devil to harass you into remaining sin conscious.

You may be struggling with certain addictive behaviors and have longed for deliverance. *Righteousness* is the key to your deliverance. Receive it. You have been equipped with righteousness, the ultimate cleansing agent, and have the right to live clean and addiction free.

My eyes began to open to this truth when I read it in Luke 10:19: "Behold, I give unto you power to tread on serpents and scorpions, and over all the power of the enemy: and nothing shall by any means hurt you." Suddenly, I realized that I am greater than the devil.

Have you received the gift of righteousness?

If you have, you should think differently, pray differently, and live differently, because you are not the same person you used to be.

RECEIVE YOUR RIGHTEOUSNESS NOW

If you will pray this prayer with me, you can put all doubt behind you and receive your righteousness. It has been yours since the day you made Jesus the Lord of your life and received Him as your personal Savior. Now is the time for you to activate your righteousness by declaring its reality.

Father, I receive your righteousness, Your free gift, into my life right now. I receive the authority that comes with being the righteousness of God in Christ, and I receive every right that has been given to me as the righteousness of God. From this day forward, I will not break agreement with Your Word. I am the righteousness of God in Christ!

Tomorrow will be a new day. Remind yourself that you not only read about the righteousness of God, but you received His righteousness. When you did, you *became* the righteousness of God.

THE COVENANT OF RIGHTEOUSNESS

CHAPTER SIX

And God said, Let us make man in our image, after our likeness: and let them have dominion over the fish of the sea, and over the fowl of the air, and over the cattle, and over all the earth, and over every creeping thing that creepeth upon the earth.

So God created man in his own image, in the image of God created he him; male and female created he them (Gen. 1:26-27).

And the Lord God formed man of the dust of the ground, and breathed into his nostrils the breath of life; and man became a living soul (Gen. 2:7).

Now the serpent was more subtle than any beast of the field which the Lord God had made. And he said unto the woman, Yea, hath God said, Ye shall not eat of every tree of the garden?

And the woman said unto the serpent, We may eat of the fruit of the trees of the garden:

But of the fruit of the tree which is in the midst of the garden, God hath said, Ye shall not eat of it, neither shall ye touch it, lest ye die.

And the serpent said unto the woman, Ye shall not surely die. (Gen. 3:1-4.)

The Bible clearly shows us how Satan always tries to contradict what God has established as truth: "For God doth know that in the day ye eat thereof, then your eyes shall be opened, and ye shall be as gods, knowing good and evil" (v. 5).

Adam and Eve were already like God. They were made in His image and likeness; they were His reflection of God on the earth. They had become living souls, just like God. They had dominion and authority over everything in the earth, as God did. Yet, the serpent contradicted that truth, and Adam did nothing about it.

It is so important to comprehend the truths God reveals about us in His Word. When we lack understanding, we can be deceived into violating His principles. That was what happened when Satan tempted Adam. It was also what Satan tried to do when he tempted Jesus.

If Adam and Eve had operated in their rights as God's creation, they would have never been deceived. We are in the same situation. By knowing who we are in Christ Jesus and operating in our rights, we cannot be defeated. We do not have to tolerate some of the things we accept.

Satan was able to mark everyone God created with the mark of sin because he had the authority from Adam to do so.

When Adam sinned, he committed high treason; treason is betrayal in its highest form.[1] God entrusted Adam with full authority as His reflection on this planet, as long as Adam was obedient to the limitations God had established: "But of the fruit of the tree which is in the midst of the garden, God hath said, Ye shall not eat of it, neither shall ye touch it, lest ye die" (Gen. 3:3).

Because Adam did not receive who he was, he accepted Eve's offer to eat of the forbidden fruit. Adam had complete authority over everything in the earth, yet he allowed Eve to convince him to do something he knew was wrong. When Adam ate the fruit, he committed treachery. He took advantage of his authority and betrayed the trust God had placed in him.

"...for in the day that thou eatest [the fruit] thou shalt surely die" (Gen. 2:17). When Adam and Eve sinned, the life of God in them and the glory of God that clothed their physical bodies departed. At that point, sin was born and everyone who was born after Adam was infected by his disobedience. (Rom. 5:12-14.)

God originally created the physical body to regenerate itself and to live forever, to exist for eternity in this physical realm. However, when Adam sinned, humankind became subject to death.

GOD'S PLAN TO RESTORE HUMANKIND

The authority God had given to Adam went all the way up to heaven, where God was seated. Adam, through disobedience, turned it over to God's enemy. God had already dealt with one traitor when He kicked Lucifer out of heaven because of his contemptuous pride. (Isa. 14:12-15.)

Having lost all place in heaven, Satan decided that if he couldn't be God, he would destroy God's plan. That is exactly what happened when Adam sinned. By disobeying God, Adam turned all his authority and dominion over to Satan. Satan did not steal it; it was given to him. It was perfectly legal because it was Adam's to give. As a result, Satan is known as the "god of this world." (2 Cor. 4:4.)

Now Satan has authority all the way from the dust of the earth up to the throne of God, but not including the throne of God. Notice, that is where Satan wanted to be. He wanted to exalt his throne above the throne of God; but thank God, there is only one Most High God.

So now everyone born of Adam is born into a sinful state regardless of who they are. (Ps. 51:5.) All are born under sin. Satan may not have been able to create or exalt himself above the throne of God, but he was able to mark everyone God created with the mark of sin because he had the authority from Adam to do so.

Now, all of humankind is born with a sin nature and is subject to death. You do not have to do anything wrong. All you have to do is be born.

This is why God had to develop a plan to redeem what was lost.

But there was a problem: Satan now had the authority and dominion once given to Adam. Therefore God was limited in how He could do things in the earth. However, God already had a way to "re-create" righteousness and bring His plan of redemption into the earth.

This is His plan:

> And I will put enmity between thee and the woman, and between thy seed and her seed; it shall bruise thy head, and thou shalt bruise his heel (Gen. 3:15).

God's plan is to originate righteousness through the seed. The sin nature began in the seed. Therefore, the solution had to come from the seed.

In order to redeem the earth, God had to get His Word into the earth. That is exactly what He did. "And the Word was made flesh, and dwelt among us..." (John 1:14). He had to find someone who would believe His Word, because if a man believed God's Word, as Adam had before he sinned, God could manifest Himself.

In Genesis 15 we find a man in idolatry, a man named Abram, whom God would later name Abraham. The righteousness Abraham received was provided to him by the covenant God established with him. Out of that covenant, righteousness was born. Genesis 15 foreshadows our connection with the righteousness we are able to receive through Jesus.

THE FATHER OF FAITH

Abram did not know about God; therefore, he had no relationship with God. In his pagan ideas, he had no knowledge of how to make contact with God. So one day God made contact with Abram.

> Abram had done nothing to deserve a visitation from God; he had done nothing to invoke the presence of God.

Abram had done nothing to deserve a visitation from God; he had done nothing to invoke the presence of God. Nevertheless, one day in a vision the Lord God spoke to Abram.

After these things the word of the Lord came unto Abram in a vision, saying, Fear not, Abram: I am thy shield, and thy exceeding great reward.

And Abram said, Lord God, what wilt thou give me, seeing I go childless, and the steward of my house is this Eliezer of Damascus?

And Abram said, Behold, to me thou hast given no seed: and, lo, one born in my house is mine heir.

And, behold, the word of the Lord came unto him, saying, This shall not be thine heir; but he that shall come forth out of thine own bowels shall be thine heir.

And he brought him forth abroad, and said, Look now toward heaven, and tell the stars, if thou be able to number them: and he said unto him, So shall thy seed be (Gen. 15:1-5).

God was making a promise.

God said that He was Abram's exceeding and great reward. He made him a father of many nations. God also gave Abram wealth and riches.

Abram responded as many of us would by asking how he would know that what God said was true. (v. 8.) It was then that God told Abram that the two of them would enter into covenant. (v. 18.)

Now, Abram may not have known God, but in his culture, when two people agreed to cut covenant, that meant the deal was signed, sealed, and as good as delivered. The purpose of this encounter with God was to once again have a righteous man in the earth. "And he believed in the Lord; and he counted it to him for righteousness" (Gen. 15:6).

Abraham had to have realized that if God told him to kill his son, then something would have to happen to cause his son to live.

The plan of redemption was underway and Abram became a righteous man because he believed. (Gen. 15:6; 17:4-5.)

He believed what God said. Then Abraham and God cut covenant to establish the Word as true, and in Abraham's mind it was settled. So finally we have a righteous man in the earth once again, and God can develop His plan for redemption.

From then on, whatever else God said, Abraham believed. He even believed and trusted God when God told him to take his son and sacrifice him. (Gen. 22:2.) Why would a man be willing to take his son up a mountain to kill him? Because God already said that Abraham would have descendents upon the earth who would outnumber the stars. Abraham believed that God would give him numerous descendants because they had cut covenant on that issue. He had to have realized that if God told him to kill his son, then something would have to happen to cause his son to live.

LAW AND ORDER

When Moses received the Ten Commandments from God on Mount Sinai, he became Israel's "lawgiver." He was already a man in covenant with God as a descendant of Abraham. When the law was given, order came into the earth.

Through Moses, God's laws are in the earth now. His covenant is in the earth. God spoke through His prophets about the plan to redeem mankind. God made a way that was perfectly legal in a fallen world to release His promise into the earth.

In Luke 1 we learn of the virgin Mary. During her time, the pattern established with Abraham was still in effect: God spoke the promise and man—or, in this case, woman—needed to agree with Him. Someone had to believe the Word in order for Jesus to be born.

The Scriptures tell us that one day an angel appeared to Mary and told her that she was highly favored of God. (Luke 1:28,30.) He also told her that she would conceive and give birth to a son. He told her that she would not know a man intimately, but the Holy Spirit would come over her and she would conceive. Believing the Word that God sent through the angel was the key to conception. (vv. 31-37.)

Mary said, "...be it unto me according to thy word..." (Luke 1:38). Once she believed it, Mary conceived Jesus by the Holy Spirit. Remember that God has to do everything legally. Satan has authority and dominion over the earth and everything and everyone in it. The only way God can move in the earth is to have someone on the earth to agree with what He says.

Jesus had to enter the world legally. He had to come in through the door to the physical world—the womb of a woman. He had to come through birth because "...he that entereth not by the door into the sheepfold, but climbeth up some other way, the same is a thief and a robber. But he that entereth in by the door is the shepherd of the sheep" (John 10:1-2).

Nine months later, God was born legally into the physical world. No longer was God only in heaven; now the Word had become flesh. As a man, He had the authority to function and operate as God in the physical world.

Here is Righteousness Himself, born in this earth as a man. However, He wasn't born in sin because He was not conceived from the seed of a man.

As Jesus grew up and began to study the Scriptures, He recognized Himself in them. Remember, Jesus was not born with all foreknowledge about His life. If He had been, He would not be our role model for the life of faith we are called to live as believers. He had to walk by faith, one step at a time, reading the Scriptures and discovering who He was. (Luke 4:16-21.)

Jesus fulfilled all righteousness when He walked the earth. (Matt. 3:15.) Here's the key: He had to die so that the righteousness He possessed could become ours once again.

> For when we were yet without strength, in due time Christ died for the ungodly (Rom. 5:6).

Jesus died for the ungodly. He died for the sinner, but when He died and His blood was shed, the righteousness of God became available to us. There has to be a connection between the righteousness of God and the death of Jesus and the shedding of that blood that makes us the righteousness of God.

> For he hath made him [Jesus] to be sin for us, who knew no sin; that we might be made the righteousness of God in him (2 Cor. 5:21).

> For since by man came death, by man came also the resurrection of the dead.

> For as in Adam all die, even so in Christ shall all be made alive (1 Cor. 15:21-22).

> That as sin hath reigned unto death, even so might grace reign through righteousness unto eternal life by Jesus Christ our Lord (Rom. 5:21 AMP).

It is through the grace of God—the gift of His righteousness—that we have eternal life. It was not easy to reestablish the righteousness of man once it was lost, but the wisdom of God prevailed.

Our covenant of righteousness is available to us through the blood of Jesus. God's righteousness is given freely to every born-again child of God. We must choose to receive His righteousness and walk in the fullness of our covenant.

REFLECTING GOD'S IMAGE

We have reached a critical point in this book. In fact, sometimes when I share this topic in church, I give people the opportunity to leave the service because I know they will be held accountable for what they hear. If they do not step into the Word they hear and do it, God says He has no choice but to judge them. (John 12:48.)

We are at that point in this book.

The next few pages will cover a revelation that, if you will sit long enough and read the conclusion of the matter, you will be a changed person. I assure you.

In proceeding, please remember several things. First, there is a difference between righteousness by faith and righteousness by works. Our righteousness is a free gift from God; we are righteous because God has declared us to be.

Here is what I consider blasphemous: the idea that you are born again but consider your-self a sinner when God says you are His righteousness.

Second, when you are the righteousness of God, it not only means that you have rights before God because of your right standing with Him; it also means you can now stand before God without the sense of guilt, condemnation, or inferiority. You can stand before God as if sin never existed.

Third, being made the righteousness of God also means you have an equality with God.

BLASPHEMY? HERESY?

If all that you are learning had been written twenty-five or thirty years ago, many would have considered these words heresy. Many would have said that it was blasphemous to declare that man has equality with God. We were always told not to compare ourselves with God. We were told that He is a holy, awesome God and we are just dirty old, good-for-nothing, undeserving sinners.

Here is what I consider blasphemous: the idea that you are born again but consider yourself a sinner when God says you are His righteousness. Your actions say to God that you really don't receive what His Word says about you.

What we must understand is that being made the righteousness of God and being like Him, having an equality with Him, is not something new. This was God's idea from the very beginning.

A REFLECTION OF GOD

Let's go even further. Genesis 1 provides an interesting aspect of the law of creation.

> And God said, let the earth bring forth the living crea-
> ture *after his kind,* cattle, and creeping thing, and beast of
> the earth *after his kind:* and it was so.
>
> And God made the beast of the earth *after his kind,*
> and cattle *after his kind,* and every thing that creepeth
> upon the earth *after his kind:* and God saw that it was good
> (Gen. 1:24-25).

Each species of livestock, wild beasts, and insects were created based on a pattern. The earth brought forth prototypes and the law of creation was set in motion.

It was no different when God created man. He subjected Himself to His own law. Genesis 1:26 says, "And God said, let us make man in our image, *after our likeness....*" We are created after God's "kind," which tells us that we are not mere human beings. Instead, we are *super*-human beings, possessing supernatural, cre-ative power. We are supernaturally created and are God-natured in spirit, soul, and body. And verse 26 let's us know that our likeness to the Father comes with dominion over His creation. This goes against what many of us have been taught.

> And God said, Let us make man in our image, after
> our likeness: and let them have dominion over the fish of
> the sea, and over the fowl of the air, and over the cattle,

and over all the earth, and over every creeping thing that creepeth upon the earth.

So God created man in his own image, in the image of God created he him; male and female created he them (Gen. 1:26-27).

When you look into the mirror, you see your reflection. If you wanted to draw or paint an image of yourself, you would look in the mirror and create the reflection you saw. God was not looking in the mirror when He said this, but in verse 26 He said that He wanted man to be a reflection of Himself.

He made us to look like and reflect His image. Not only was humankind to look like and reflect God's image, but to be like Him in character.

And the Lord God formed man of the dust of the ground, and breathed into his nostrils the breath of life; and man became a living soul (Gen. 2:7).

A SPEAKING SPIRIT

The Chumash translates Genesis 2:7 this way: "God breathed into the nostrils of man, and man became another speaking spirit."[1] That is an accurate translation of this verse because God said, "…Let us make man in our image…" (Gen. 1:26). God is a Spirit. So if man is made in His image, then man is a spirit. God is a speaking Spirit. Therefore, if we are made like Him, we have to speak as well.

When God made Adam, He made an exact duplicate of Himself. God was the original image, and from His image He created another image of Himself—the man Adam.

It's important to understand that you are not second-class. You are an exact duplicate of the image of God. This does not mean that you are God. It means that you are made in God's image and His likeness, with an ability to create with words as God did.

WHY DO I NEED A BODY?

Man is a three-part being. He is a *spirit*, who possesses a *soul*, and who lives in a *body*. (1 Thess. 5:23.) You cannot have dominion in this physical world without a physical suit. Your earth suit, your body, is not you; it is just an outfit.

When we die and leave this world, our earth suits (our bodies) remain. It's just like removing your clothes, and watching them fall to the floor. As long as you're in that suit, it has movement. Likewise, when our earth suit dies, our soul returns to heaven and the earth suit becomes lifeless.

Now, you do not *have* a spirit; you *are* a spirit made in the image of God. Remember, you are another "speaking spirit."

> This is the book of the generations of Adam. In the day that God created man, in the likeness of God made he him.
>
> Male and female created he them; and blessed them... (Gen. 5:1).

If man was created in the likeness of God, then that means there are similarities between the two.

Say this out loud. *I am like God.*

> And the Lord God formed man of the dust of the ground, and breathed into his nostrils the breath of life; and man became a living soul (Gen. 2:7).

He formed the body of a man out of the dust, but the body was lifeless. The Bible says that God *breathed* into the nostrils of man.

HE SPOKE LIFE

I used to envision God giving Adam's lifeless body a form of CPR, putting His mouth up to Adam's nostrils and blowing. But that is not what happened. Remember, God breathed life into this entire planet.

Notice what happens when you speak. Every time you speak words, you are breathing at the same time.

It is up to us to lay hold of our godship.

Adam's body was formed from the dust, but it was not alive. Just as God spoke forth light and the firmament, He spoke forth man, and man became a living soul. (Gen. 2:7.)

God took a reflection of Himself and placed it in a physical body formed out of the dust. Then He breathed His own life into it, named him Adam, and gave him authority over all physical things on the planet. God in heaven had made Adam god of the earth. Adam was crowned god of all physical things formed from the dust of the earth: "Let him have dominion" (Gen. 1:26). That included dominion over the moon, the stars, and the planets.

GUARDIAN OF CREATION

All of God's handiwork was now placed in the authority of the god of the earth—Adam. Then God told Adam to guard the Garden of Eden and keep out all intruders. (Gen. 2:15 AMP.)

Now, that gives us a little insight into why God wanted a god on the earth like He was God in heaven. Lucifer was an intruder who had tried to take over heaven and had now set his sights on the earth.

God has always designed a reflection of Himself on this planet because the earth is a reflection of heaven. It is up to us to lay hold of our godship.

And out of the ground the Lord God formed every beast of the field, and every fowl of the air; and brought them unto Adam to see what he would call them: and whatsoever Adam called every living creature, that was the name thereof.

And Adam gave names to all cattle, and to the fowl of the air, and to every beast of the field (Gen. 2:19-20).

Notice again, God formed the physical bodies of the animals out of the ground just as He had Adam, but nowhere do we find

God breathing life into them. They did not have life until Adam spoke words of life over them.

God was training a god in the earth. He had to teach him how to do what He does. This god would have authority over the animals. The reason he would have authority over the animals is that they would not live until he gave them life, just as God had given Adam life.

> And out of the ground the Lord God formed every beast of the field, and every fowl of the air; and brought them unto Adam to see what he would call them... (Gen. 2:19).

God formed Adam's physical body out of the dust of the ground and called him into existence. He then showed Adam to do what He did, including how to use the power of his words. When Adam said, "Buffalo," the buffalo came to life. He was breathing life into that which he had authority over through the spoken word.

God called it, and it was. Adam called it, and it was—just as if God Himself had called it. Adam had authority. He was god of this physical realm just as God was God of the spiritual realm. Adam was god of this planet and all the handiwork of God.

The book of James talks about this as well.

> [With the tongue] bless we God, even the Father; and therewith curse we men, which are made after the similitude (or likeness) of God (James 3:9).

Even James declares that we have been made similar to, and in the likeness of, God.

In Psalm 8 David writes:

> What is man, that thou art mindful of him? and the son
> of man, that thou visitest him?

> For thou hast made him a little lower than the angels,
> and hast crowned him with glory and honour (Ps. 8:4-5).

In the Hebrew Bible, the word for "angel" is *Elohim.*[1] *Elohim* is the name of God that describes Him as the Creator of all physical things. The psalmist is saying that man was made a little lower than *Elohim,* the Creator of all physical things.

The reason the psalmist used the word *Elohim* is that this is how man was made. One part of man that is like God is the creative part: the ability to speak and to create. That's why our confessions are so important. There is creative ability in our words, and we have the ability to create good or evil with our words. "Death and life are in the power of the tongue..." (Prov. 18:21).

ADOPTED AS A SON

The Bible says Jesus was the only begotten Son of God. (John 3:16.) To become a son of God, one must be adopted into His family.

> But when the fulness of time was come, God sent forth
> his Son, made of a woman, made under the law,

> To redeem them that were under the law, that we
> might receive the adoption of sons (Gal. 4:4-5).

Adoption is a legal process that makes someone else's child part of your family and equal with your natural children in rights and privileges. In the natural, there is an equality that comes through adoption.

In Galatians 4:4-5, Paul is saying that the same thing has happened to believers: We received the adoption of sons when we were born again.

If we are sons and daughters of God, and Jesus is *the* Son of God, then that makes us equal to and joint-heirs with Jesus.

When asked, many of us will say we believe we are sons and daughters of God. We became sons and daughters of God when we were adopted into the family of God the day we became born again.

If we are sons and daughters of God, and Jesus is *the* Son of God, then that makes us equal to and joint-heirs with Jesus. (Rom. 8:16-17.) Remember, adoption makes us family with equal rights. It makes us, in a sense, equal to Jesus, who is God.

You are the image of God. Even if you were hurt, that does not change who you are. Like many, you may have been raised without an earthly father. Still, that does not change who you are.

Don't allow negative life experiences to sabotage your future in Jesus. If anything, those experiences should make you more determined than ever to be everything God intends you to be.

But Jesus answered them, My Father worketh hitherto, and I work.

Therefore the Jews sought the more to kill him, because he not only had broken the sabbath, but said also that God was his Father, making himself equal with God (John 5:17-18).

The Jews understood that when one called God "Father," he was saying he was a son and had equality with God. So when Jesus called God His Father, they tried to stone Him. Like Jesus, there is a price to pay once you declare that you share equality with God. You may be rejected and outcast from certain circles of friends. Don't compromise your righteousness stance. Remain true to who you are in God.

YOU ARE "GODS"

How long will you [magistrates or judges] judge unjustly and show partiality to the wicked?....

Do justice to the weak (poor) and fatherless; maintain the rights of the afflicted and needy.

Deliver the poor and needy; rescue them out of the hand of the wicked.

[The magistrates and judges] know not, neither will they understand; they walk on in the darkness [of complacent satisfaction]; all the foundations of the earth [the fundamental principles upon which rests the administration of justice] are shaking.

I said, You are gods [since you judge on My behalf, as My representatives]; indeed, all of you are children of the Most High (Ps. 82:2-6 AMP).

Verse 6 says, "I said, You are gods...[and] all of you are children of the Most High God." In this context, verse 6 means,

"Because you speak for Me as magistrates and judges, you are gods." The casual reader would think, *Certainly this doesn't mean we are really gods.*

Something very interesting happens in John 10. The Pharisees are preparing to stone Jesus, not because of any of the miracles He has done, but for another very interesting reason.

> Jesus answered them, Many good works have I shown you from my Father; for which of those good works do ye stone me?
>
> The Jews answered him, saying, For a good work we stone thee not; but for blasphemy; and because that thou, being a man, makest thyself God (John 10:32-33).

The Jews did not want to stone Him because of His good works. They wanted to stone Him because they considered His words to be blasphemy.

> Jesus answered them, Is it not written in your law, I said, Ye are gods (John 10:34)?

Here, Jesus is not talking about judges and magistrates.

> If [God] called them gods, unto whom the word of God came, and the scripture cannot be broken;
>
> Say ye of him, whom the Father hath sanctified, and sent into the world, Thou blasphemest; because I said, I am the Son of God (John 10:35-36)?

Jesus understood the equality and the similarity man has with God, that we are created a little lower than *Elohim*. He understands in whose image He is created; Jesus knows where He came from.

I AM NOT GOD, AND NEITHER ARE YOU

Here is the understanding you should receive concerning this chapter. It's understood that you or I are not God. There is only one God. However, as His children, we are like Him. He's the big "G," and we're the little "g." In Him we have been given the authority to rule and reign in this earth just as Jesus did. We have the mind of Christ. Even Jesus said that we would do the works He did and greater works as well. (John 14:12.)

If I do not the works of my Father, believe me not.

But if I do, though ye believe not me, believe the works: that ye may know, and believe, that the Father is in me, and I in him (John 10:37-38).

Jesus was warning us not to stumble over what He has said about Himself.

It is not going to be enough for you to go around saying that you are the image and likeness of God, or that you are just like Jesus. When you start performing the works of the Father, others are going to know that there is something unique about you. People will believe and see your testimony as a son or daughter of God because of the events that surround your life.

We are not studying this teaching on how we reflect the image of God simply so we can do and say things as Jesus did and said things. Yes, we want results; we should expect just what Jesus expected. However, there continues to be a fear among Christians: the fear of walking like a son or a daughter of God.

We need to say to that fear, "Be gone!" and wake up the sleeping giant inside of you.

Lift your hands up and say out loud: *I receive now the grace of God that gives me my righteousness. I declare that I am the righteousness of God. I am the image of God. I'm just like Jesus. I believe it. I receive it and now I establish myself in this truth. In Jesus' mighty name I pray, Amen.*

When I completed this teaching on righteousness at church, a lady approached the altar and dropped her crutch. When I asked her what she felt and what had happened, she replied, "I'm just like Jesus. I'll never be sick another day in my life. I'll never be depressed. I'll never be down another day in my life. I now know who I am."

ACCEPTING YOUR INHERITANCE

CHAPTER EIGHT

I know the previous chapter was a lot to take in. It was for me too. However, now that I know who I am and the authority God has given me to rule in this world, I am better able to carry out His plan for my life. Trust me, the last thing the devil wants you to do is get a hold of who you are in Christ Jesus. Read what follows with thoughtful intent.

> For ye have not received the spirit of bondage again to fear; but ye have received the Spirit of adoption, whereby we cry, Abba, Father (Rom. 8:15).

The day you were born again and put on Christ, you became just like Him. Romans 8:16-17 says, "The Spirit itself beareth witness with our spirit, that we are the children of God: And if children, then heirs."

93

When you put on righteousness, you put on sonship.

Do you really believe you are a son of God? You are if you have made Jesus your Lord and Savior. That makes you an heir. Sons become heirs. Since you are an heir, you have an inheritance. You are an adopted son and therefore equal with Jesus.

> *In the righteousness of God, you are just like Jesus. You have been adopted into a royal family.*

And if we are [His] children, then we are [His] heirs also: heirs of God and fellow heirs with Christ [sharing His inheritance with Him]; only we must share His suffering if we are to share His glory (Rom. 8:17 AMP).

Now, a joint heir is an equal heir. Joint heirs share equally in an inheritance. Being a joint heir with Christ means we do not lack anything Jesus has. His righteousness entitled Him to everything He has, and His righteousness entitles us to everything He has. Our adoption as sons makes us joint heirs.

Now go back to verse 15. *The Amplified Bible* says:

> For [the Spirit which] you now have received [is] not a spirit of slavery to put you once more in bondage to fear, but you have received the Spirit of adoption [the Spirit producing sonship] (Rom. 8:15).

The day you were born again, you were adopted as a child of God into the family of God. Your adoption made it possible for you to put on the righteousness of God and become a joint heir with Jesus. You became just like Jesus in the eyes of the Father.

Say this out loud: *I am just like Jesus.* That is hard to take in, isn't it?

The devil might attempt to deceive you by saying that you cannot be just like Jesus because you sinned at some point in your life. That is your opportunity to declare that you are the righteousness of God and therefore just like Jesus.

Do you remember what the apostle Paul said? You may remember that he was the one who persecuted Christians and delivered them up to be killed, the one who stood holding the coats of those who were stoning Stephen. Long after his conversion on the road to Damascus he said, "...we have wronged no man..." (2 Cor. 7:2).

How could he have said that after all he had done? He knew what it was to stand in the righteousness of God; therefore, he could declare with a clean conscience that he was the righteousness of God. You can also declare that in the righteousness of God, you have wronged no man. In the righteousness of God, you are just like Jesus. You have been adopted into a royal family. You come from the household of Jesus.

In Jesus we are like Him. In Him we are joint heirs with Him. In Him we can lay hands on the sick and see them recover. In Him we can raise the dead. In Him we can multiply food. I have seen mothers do it when nothing was in the pantry: stand in faith believing, praying, and thanking God. Then the doorbell rings and someone is standing there with two sacks of groceries.

IN HIM

This is not some second-class righteousness. Jesus does not have one type of righteousness and you have another kind. The righteousness of God you have is just like Jesus' righteousness. Your ability to heal others is just like Jesus' ability. The anointing on you is just like Jesus' anointing. If you begin to accept your identity in Jesus, you will also begin to operate just as He did.

In the past we have had a lot of enthusiasm for God, but it has not been enlightened or according to [correct and vital] knowledge. (Rom. 10:2 AMP.)

It is absolutely God's will for you to be just like Jesus. That is what God has wanted you to understand and accept the whole time. He wants you to walk in this truth so that Satan cannot talk you out of your inheritance as a joint heir.

But when the fulness of the time was come, God sent forth his Son, made of a woman, made under the law,

To redeem them that were under the law, that we might receive the adoption of sons.

And because ye are sons, God hath sent forth the Spirit of his Son into your hearts, crying, Abba, Father (Gal. 4:4-6).

In other words, now that you are a son or daughter of God, you have His Spirit in your heart. When you realize this truth, you will cry, "Abba Father," or "Daddy."

If you do not think He is your Father, you will say "God." I am a son, and I never called my Daddy by His first name.

HEIRS AND INHERITANCE

Now, let's talk about being heirs and about our inheritance.

For as many as are led by the Spirit of God, they are the sons of God.

For ye have not received the spirit of bondage again to fear; but ye have received the Spirit of adoption, whereby we cry, Abba, Father.

The Spirit itself beareth witness with our spirit, that we are the children of God:

And if children, then heirs; heirs of God, and joint-heirs with Christ" (Rom. 8:14-17).

When you adopt a child, that child receives your name and your inheritance. That child becomes your heir. However, in order to receive his inheritance, he must begin to act in accordance with the customs, rules, or behavior of the family. In other words, he must conform to his new family and leave his old family behind.

We are heirs of God. As heirs, a portion of everything your father has is going to be yours. As joint heirs with Christ, we share the same rights as Jesus.

ONE FOR ALL, ALL FOR ONE

For as many of you as have been baptized into Christ have put on Christ.

There is neither Jew nor Greek (nor black, nor white, nor Hispanic, nor Asian, nor Indian), there is neither bond nor free, there is neither male nor female: for ye are all one in Christ Jesus (Gal. 3:27-28).

Sadly, there is racism in the Body of Christ. How can racism exist when we are all equal in Him? How can there be racism when as members of the same family we are all conformed to Him?

The Church is always talking about, "Until we become one…." We are one already. We just don't act like it. Jesus died One for all. Our attitude as family should be all for One and One for all.

Our responsibility as family members is to have an attitude of all for One.

We are never going to become one in life until we receive our righteousness and realize that, as adopted sons, we all conform to the same family. When I am in His righteousness, I will not judge you when you miss the mark, because I know that correction is simply getting back into His righteousness. If I am in His righteousness, I no longer judge you by the flesh. I see you as conformed to the Father God.

I can no longer see you by the color of your skin, by how much you earn a year, or by where you grew up.

NO LONGER A SERVANT

Wherefore thou art no more a servant, but a son; and if a son, then an heir of God through Christ (Gal. 4:7).

Notice the Scripture says that you are no longer servants.

Moses was a servant. Elijah was a servant. Read the Old Testament, and you will see what God did for His servants. If He did all that for His servants, just imagine what He is willing to do for His sons.

In fact, He has already done everything for His sons and daughters He intends to do. Now He is trying to get us to accept our rightful position with Him. You might be tempted to think, *I am just a Christian. Jesus is the Son.* No, Jesus was the firstborn; and if there were not going to be a second-born or third-born, Jesus would not be referred to as the firstborn of many brethren. (Rom. 8:29.) Jesus was the firstborn of many brethren, of which I am one. So are you if you are born again.

Settle that here and now. You are a son of God. Our relationship with Abba transcends gender, so both men and women have the right of inheritance.

NOT SERVANTS, BUT SONS

But when the fulness of the time was come, God sent forth his Son, made of a woman, made under the law,

To redeem them that were under the law, that we might receive the adoption of sons.

And because ye are sons, God hath sent forth the Spirit of his Son into your hearts, crying, Abba, Father.

Wherefore thou art no more a servant, but a son; and if a son, then an heir of God through Christ (Gal. 4:4-7).

Sons can do what servants cannot do. But servants only do what they are told to do. I am a son.

I used to say that I was a servant of God because it sounded good, but God told me not to say that anymore. He said that I am a son.

What's the difference?

Sons act like their fathers.

THINK LIKE THIS

Let this mind [this attitude] be in you, which was also in Christ Jesus:

Who, being in the form of God, thought it not robbery to be equal with God (Phil. 2:5-6).

This Scripture says that even though Jesus had taken on the form of a man, He did not consider it an act of robbery to think of Himself as equal with God. He advises us to have the same mindset.

Even though you are in this world, do not think you are robbing God of anything when you think of yourself as Jesus did. It is not only okay, but it is God's desire. The more we think like Jesus did, the more He can accomplish in the earth.

THE FAITH COMMAND

Why does He want this attitude of equality with the Son of God to be in you?

That ye may be blameless and harmless, the sons of God, without rebuke, in the midst of a crooked and perverse nation, among whom ye shine as lights in the world (Phil. 2:15).

At first, I felt uncomfortable exercising my rights as Jesus did. The people around me thought I was strange. They thought I was crazy when I spoke to storms. They thought I was crazy when I visited someone in the hospital and told cancer to leave them, or when I called money to come into my household.

Yet this question kept coming to my mind: *Why would Jesus give me all authority in heaven and in earth if I were not supposed to exercise it? In addition, if I am supposed to exercise that authority, why would it be wrong to expect that the circumstances obey me?*

In most cases, it is not that the circumstances do not obey us, but, because we think so little of ourselves as born-again believers, we seldom give the faith command. We seldom exercise our God-given rights because we think, *I'm simply a human being. He is a big, huge God,* and we pray prayers like "If it be Thy will, O God...."

Does this sound like you?

TRANSFERRED INTO HIS KINGDOM

Giving thanks unto the Father, which hath made us meet (able or qualified) to be partakers of the inheritance of the saints in light:

Who hath delivered us from the power of darkness, and hath translated (or transferred) us into the kingdom of his dear Son (Col. 1:12-13).

We have been transferred. The same way someone is transferred out of the maintenance department into the accounting department or from the marketing department to advertising, we have been transferred.

We have also been transferred out of sickness into healing, out of poverty into prosperity, and out of addiction into deliverance. Through Jesus, we have been transferred out of our circumstance into the good life.

Let's look into the Scripture to see exactly who Jesus is.

THIS JESUS

In whom we have redemption through his blood, even the forgiveness of sins:

Who is the image of the invisible God, the firstborn of every creature:

For by him were all things created, that are in heaven, and that are in earth, visible and invisible, whether they be thrones, or dominions, or principalities, or powers: all things were created by him, and for him:

And he is before all things, and by him all things consist.

And he is the head of the body, the church: who is the beginning, the firstborn from the dead; that in all things he might have preeminence.

For it pleased the Father that in him should all fulness dwell;

And, having made peace through the blood of his cross, by him to reconcile all things unto himself; by him, I say, whether they be things in earth, or things in heaven.

And you, that were sometime alienated and enemies in your mind by wicked works, yet now hath he reconciled in the body of his flesh through death, to present you holy and unblameable and unreproveable in His sight (Col. 1:14-22).

Everything Jesus did and He went through, was so that you and I could be clothed in His righteousness and presented as holy and spotless in the sight of God Almighty. The result is that we are thereby reconciled to God.

However, there is a condition: *You must continue in the faith.* It is not enough to read or even understand it. It is not enough to shout about it or even tell everyone you know. You must receive it by faith and continue in it.

HIS GREAT LOVE

Behold, what manner of love the Father hath bestowed upon us, that we should be called the sons of God: therefore the world knoweth us not, because it knew him not (1 John 3:1).

Look at that love. God chose us and called us His sons. Before we were saved, some of us were good-for-nothing, lying, double-talking, hedonistic, if-it-feels-good-do-it sinners and proud of it. Others were trying to be good and battling sin nature every day. Some of us were both. Nevertheless, we were all headed in the same direction—death and hell. Yet God received us all when we cried out for a Savior. That is the love of God made manifest to us.

> Beloved, now are we the sons of God, and it doth not yet appear what we shall be: but we know that, when he shall appear, we shall be like him; for we shall see him as he is (1 John 3:2).

When I see Him, I know I am going to be just like Jesus—and He is going to be just like me. As far as our righteousness is concerned, we are identical twins.

YOU HAVE BEEN PROMOTED

> John to the seven churches which are in Asia: Grace be unto you, and peace, from him which is, and which was, and which is to come; and from the seven Spirits, which are before his throne;

> And from Jesus Christ, who is the faithful witness, and the first begotten of the dead, and the prince of the kings of the earth. Unto him that loved us, and washed us from our sins in his own blood,

> And hath made us kings and priests unto God and His Father... (Rev. 1:4-6).

The Scripture says that you are a king.

Every king has a kingdom. God cannot make you king and not give you a kingdom. The Bible says, "...the kingdom of God is within you" (Luke 17:21). So the kingdom is wherever the king is.

God has made you a king. Not only that, He has also made you a priest. The job of a priest is to mediate between God and man. This is what He meant when He said we have been given both the word and the ministry of reconciliation.

> And all things are of God, who hath reconciled us to himself by Jesus Christ, and hath given to us the ministry of reconciliation;
>
> To wit, that God was in Christ, reconciling the world unto himself, not imputing their trespasses unto them; and hath committed unto us the word of reconciliation (2 Cor. 5:18-19).

So, how are we going to do this new job into which we have been promoted? To do any job well, a person must have two things: full responsibility and full authority. That is why you are both a king and a priest. As a priest you have the responsibility, and as a king you have the authority.

THE MESSAGE

Here is the message we have to declare:

> Therefore as by the offence of one judgment came upon all men to condemnation; even so by the righteous-ness of one the free gift (of righteousness) came upon all men unto justification of life.

For as by one man's disobedience many were made sinners, so by the obedience of one shall many be made righteous (Rom. 5:18-19).

Because of Jesus, we have the free gift of righteousness. Because of Adam, sin came into the world. But because of Jesus, righteousness came. People were born into the world as sinners and shaped into iniquity; but now, if we believe and receive this free gift of righteousness, then we can become the righteousness of God.

Therefore if any man be in Christ, he is a new creature: old things are passed away; behold, all things are become new.

Now then we are ambassadors for Christ, as though God did beseech you (beg you) by us: we pray you in Christ's stead, be ye reconciled to God.

For he hath made him to be sin for us, who knew no sin; that we might be made the righteousness of God in him (2 Cor. 5:17,20,21).

Say it out loud so you can hear it. Declare the truth of what was provided for you when Jesus died: *I am the righteousness of God.*

Does the righteousness of God have a part with unrighteousness? No. Saying, "I am a sinner saved by grace," is an attempt to partner sin with the righteousness of God. There is no partnership between the two. You are either righteous or a sinner. It is up to you to choose.

When you are the righteousness of God, you are not a sinner saved by grace. You *were* a sinner, but since you've been born again, that nature is nowhere to be found in you.

It cannot be denied that we all miss the mark sometimes, but as the righteousness of God we have a right to partake of the advocate ministry of Jesus and receive our cleansing and forgiveness. (1 John 1:9.) You do not partner with unrighteousness.

Sinners practice sin. Righteousness-of-God people practice their rights, which may be, in some cases, the right to be cleansed from sin. But if you awaken to righteousness, you will sin not. (1 Cor. 15:34.) I am convinced, not only by my own experience but by what believers who have heard this teaching tell me, that the more conscious you become of your righteousness, the less you will sin and the less you will want to.

> The more conscious you become of your righteousness, the less you will sin and the less you will want to.

THE PROMISE YOU CAN COUNT ON

Here is what *Jesus* said before He died:

Blessed are they which do hunger and thirst after righteousness: for they shall be filled (Matt. 5:6).

Since I began teaching righteousness, I have received some interesting reactions. People wonder what will happen to their lives if they really begin to establish themselves in righteousness.

I understand the concern. I know this is a radical understanding of our relationship with Jesus and God. But, it's biblical. It's right there in black, white, and most importantly, red.

If you really step into the righteousness of God it will become an unstoppable force in your life. You will begin to dominate and rule every circumstance in your life. More than just an identity, it will become a force for good to produce everything you need, i.e., food, clothes, protection, and guidance.

Jesus used light and darkness to talk about righteousness and unrighteousness.

More than just an identity, righteousness will become a force for good to produce everything you need.

Then spake Jesus again unto them, saying, I am the light of the world: he that followeth me shall not walk in darkness, but shall have the light of life (John 8:12).

When you are established in righteousness and following Jesus, you have His personal assurance that you will not walk in darkness but will have the way made clear to you.

I have said all of this so you will know that the inheritance Jesus has provided for you in Him can be yours if you will establish yourself in His righteousness. It is not as easy as simply saying that you believe. It has to sink down deep into your spirit. It has to become your identity, as well as your motivation, your inclination, and your automatic response to any situation and person.

That means you may have to read this book repeatedly to fully understand the message. You may even need to read it out loud to yourself.

It will take a commitment on your part to become established in this teaching. Nothing else works until this is established. Just as you cannot build a house without a foundation, you cannot experience the power of God in your life and the richness of the relationship with Him you desire until you become established in your righteousness in Christ.

Becoming conformed to the word of righteousness is the process that helps to make you an heir, as examined in the next chapter.

CONFORMED TO THE FAMILY

We are a reflection of God Himself. We stand as equals with Jesus. Declare out loud: *I have an equality with God.* You may be thinking, *I am not going to say that. I am not going to even think it.*

When you stand in the righteousness of God, you stand in everything He is, everything He has, and in the very same anointing He possesses! You will rise far above where you are right now when you lay hold of that fact.

However, we do not think like this in order to become arrogant and rude.

[Jesus] made himself of no reputation, and took upon him the form of a servant, and was made in the likeness of men:

111

And being found in fashion as a man, he humbled himself, and became obedient unto death, even the death of the cross (Phil. 2:7-8).

When you stand in the righteousness of God, you stand in everything He is, everything He has, and every anointing He possesses!

Understand there was a process that had to take place, even with Jesus. When He was born, He was just like you and me. He had to study the Scriptures and discover who He was in God's eyes just as we must do. The only difference between Jesus and the rest of us is that He didn't have a sin nature to distract Him.

For thirty years, Jesus was immersed in the Scriptures until He had conformed Himself to the Word of God. He studied the Word and found Himself in the Scriptures. He meditated on that Word day and night and became what He meditated.

Jesus knew without a shadow of doubt that He was the Messiah, and He had heard the audible voice of God say, "This is My beloved Son." He knew He was a man, yet He also understood that He was equal with God. Therefore, He could stand before a grave and say, "Lazarus come forth!" and know that Lazarus would come forth. (John 11:43.) He had received His rights as the Son of God.

In fact, when He went to the tomb of Lazarus to raise him from the dead, He already knew what the Father was going to do. But for the sake of those around Him, He called Lazarus by name so that they would believe.

If only we would meditate in the Word of righteousness until we reached a point of conforming ourselves to it and believing it without doubt. If we did that, we would start identifying our rights, taking hold of our rights, walking in our rights, speaking our rights, and seeing them come to pass.

Then we could say that we are just like Jesus.

Do you know why Jesus could walk through an angry mob of people who wanted to throw Him off the cliff and escape without a scratch? He could do that because He knew who He was. He knew that they could not defeat Him. He had been meditating in the Word for thirty years, and He knew they could not distract Him, neither could they destroy the purpose for His life. They wanted to, but they were not successful.

MADE TO BE

"For he hath made him to be sin for us...." Jesus was made to be sin, because without a sin nature, He never committed sin. "...That we might be made the righteousness of God in Him" (2 Cor. 5:21).

Although Jesus never sinned, there was an exchange that took place on the cross. He removed His righteousness and put on our sin nature. That allowed him legal access to hell in order to set those in captivity free. Just as one must be made righteous in order to enter heaven, one must be made sin to enter hell legally. Hence, the need for Jesus to be made sin in order to redeem those in captivity and those destined for hell. Then He was raised from the dead and put on righteousness once again making us, who knew no righteousness, the righteousness of God.

UNEQUALLY YOKED

Second Corinthians 6:14 says, "Be ye not unequally yoked together with unbelievers." How ridiculous would it be to talk about inequality if equality did not exist?

> Wherefore come out from among them, and be ye separate, saith the Lord, and touch not the unclean thing;
>
> And I will receive you, and will be a Father unto you, and ye shall be my sons and daughters, saith the Lord Almighty (2 Cor. 6:17-18).

We are more than unclean, undeserving, unworthy, filthy rags. We are sons and daughters of the Most High God, and it is time for us to conform to who we really are!

A very good question comes up at this point: What happens if we continue to refuse to conform to His righteousness as born-again believers? What are the consequences of continuing to value ourselves according to our own righteousness instead of God's?

If you continue to speak or act as though the blood of Jesus is insufficient, and as though you are unworthy, the Word says it will be accounted to you as sin.

> For if after they have escaped the pollutions of the world through the knowledge of the Lord and Saviour Jesus Christ, they are again entangled therein, and overcome, the latter end is worse with them than the beginning.
>
> For it had been better for them not to have known the way of righteousness, than, after they have known it, to turn

from the holy commandment delivered unto them (2 Peter 2:20-21).

You would have been better off without the knowledge than to hear the way of righteousness and turn away from it.

> Howbeit then, when ye knew not God, ye did service unto them which by nature are no gods (Gal. 4:8).

You were in bondage to false gods, who by their very nature could not be gods at all.

> But now, after that ye have known God, or rather are known [by] God, how turn ye again to the weak and beggarly elements, whereunto ye desire again to be in bondage (Gal. 4:9)?

> I am alarmed [about you], lest I have labored among and over you to no purpose and in vain (Gal. 4:11 AMP).

If we are told about the righteousness of God and still choose to live in sin, we only prove that we are satisfied in defeat, poverty, and sickness.

> For if we sin willfully after that we have received the knowledge of the truth [about the righteousness of God], there remaineth no more sacrifice for sins,

> But a certain fearful looking for of judgment and fiery indignation, which shall devour the adversaries.

> He that despised Moses' law died without mercy under two or three witnesses: of how much sorer punish-

ment, suppose ye, shall he be thought worthy, who hath trodden under foot the Son of God, and hath counted the blood of the covenant, wherewith he was sanctified, an unholy thing, and hath done despite unto the Spirit of grace (Heb. 10:26-29)?

Jesus shed His blood and submitted His body as the final sacrifice for our redemption. He desires to give you a gift so that you can be just like Him. It would be an insult to reject it because you think you are unworthy.

It is no different than if you win a court case in which you are facing life in prison, and the judge pardons you and sets you free. It would not make any sense for you to refuse your freedom and insist on going to jail.

There are many that feel they have to go through something before they can feel worthy enough to be forgiven.

Forgiving yourself is important. But the biggest issue is receiving God's forgiveness. How can you otherwise forgive yourself of your own sins?

BEFORE YOU RECEIVE YOUR INHERITANCE

When my father was hospitalized, I was given power of attorney on his behalf. I paid his bills by writing a check on his account, signing my name. The bank honored the check as though it were my father's. When he died, I became the legal guardian of all my father's personal matters. I did not receive that authority, however, until my father had died.

In John 16:7 Jesus said, "…It is expedient for you that I go away: for if I go not away, the Comforter will not come unto you; but if I depart, I will send him unto you."

In other words, Jesus was saying that it was to their advantage that He go away, because as long as He was present, they could not receive the Holy Spirit. When Jesus departed, they not only received power and authority to act just like Him, but they also were able to operate under the same power and authority. This power is available to everyone who receives His righteousness.

Jesus said in John 16:8 that the Holy Spirit would come to reprove the world of three things: sin, righteousness, and judgment. Sin because they did not believe on Jesus. Righteousness because Jesus is going to the Father, and judgment because the prince of this world, Satan, has already been judged. (vv. 9-11.) Jesus has already returned to His heavenly Father. It is all taken care of. It is now the job of the Holy Spirit, along with the Word of God, to convince humankind of this truth.

> Jesus said in John 16:8 that the Holy Spirit would come to reprove the world of three things: sin, righteousness, and judgment.

We cannot ignore this truth and attempt to relate to God based on religious traditions. We don't have to earn our righteousness. When we lay hold of our position in the righteousness of God, we allow the Holy Spirit to conform us by faith to the image we were re-created in: the image of a son, the image of an heir.

OPPORTUNITY LOST

Consider what would have happened if the Church had wrapped its arms around the televangelists who fell during the late 1980s and 90s. What if they were told that despite their sin, they had a right to be forgiven by God because of their identity in Christ as righteous people. Consider what kind of power those men might have had on their lives today.

Have you received your righteousness by faith? Have you allowed the Holy Spirit the liberty to work in your life to conform you to the image of your spiritual family?

You are the righteousness of God, and from this day forward you must make a conscious decision to renew your mind. It's important to discern how religion has distorted a truth that was supposed to be the centerpiece for everything we do. You have to allow the Spirit of God to conform you to His Word and dismiss any feelings of unworthiness.

Here's your declaration: *In the name of Jesus, I declare that I am just like Jesus. I am an heir of God, a joint heir with Christ Jesus. I am the righteousness of God right now; and I ask You, Father, to conform me to the Word of Your righteousness. I receive that! In Jesus' name.*

CHANGE YOUR DIRECTION

Understanding sin in light of our righteousness will add balance to this revelation. Sin is not a problem to God, but it could be a problem to us.

What I don't want to happen is for someone to finish this book and think to himself, *I can live any way I choose because the righteousness of God will cover it all.* The entire point would have been missed. We need a clear understanding of just how powerful our position is in righteousness.

One of the things I have said repeatedly is that righteousness is the ability to stand before God without the sense of guilt, condemnation, or inferiority.

We have discovered that we have equality with God. The Bible says Jesus "thought it not robbery to [see himself] equal with God" (Phil. 2:6). When we are in Him, we cannot think it robbery to see ourselves like Him. As long as we are in Him, we are like Him.

THE FREE GIFT OF RIGHTEOUSNESS

We understand righteousness as a gift of God to be received by faith. Man does not work for righteousness, because it is a gift. It is something you receive, not something you earn.

> For what saith the scripture? Abraham believed God, and it was counted unto him for righteousness.
>
> Now to him that worketh is the reward not reckoned of grace, but of debt.
>
> But to him that worketh not, but believeth on him that justifieth the ungodly, his faith is counted for righteousness (Rom. 4:3-5).

Your righteousness is in Him and not in your works.

Works will only be a stumbling stone in your path because righteousness must be received by faith. The moment you believe and receive Jesus as your Lord and personal Savior, your faith in what the blood of Jesus has accomplished for you was released. God releases the free gift of righteousness

120

into your life and you become the righteousness of God in Christ. You cannot earn it. God makes you His righteousness.

LIVING BY FAITH IN YOUR RIGHTEOUSNESS

Hebrews 10:38 says, "Now the just shall live by faith...." Therefore, those of us who have been declared righteous have a prescribed way to live our lives, according to the Bible.

Often we think we know how the Bible is instructing us to live. But truthfully, many principles have been taken out of their proper context. Much of what has been learned is wrong because it was taken from religious tradition rather than looking at it in light of the righteousness of God.

> Therefore being justified [or declared righteous] by faith, we have peace [or wholeness] with God through our Lord Jesus Christ:

> By whom also we have access by faith into this grace [the righteousness of God] wherein we stand, and rejoice in hope of the glory of God (Rom. 5:1-2).

Because we have been declared righteous, we are at peace with God. Once you receive your righteousness, it is time to rejoice because you are standing in your right to have everything that the Bible says you are entitled to. Now that I am righteous, I have a right to see things change in my life.

PATIENCE: A FRUIT OF RIGHTEOUSNESS

And not only so, but we glory in tribulations also: knowing that tribulation worketh patience;

And patience [worketh], experience; and experience [worketh], hope (Rom. 5:3).

This Scripture has been preached out of context for a very long time.

Remember, we are talking about righteousness. Even when problems occur, we will be all right if we stand in our righteousness.

Notice this little phrase: Knowing that tribulation worketh patience. If you are not careful, you will conclude that tribulation produces patience. That is not true. If tribulation produced patience, the world would be full of patient people.

Most of us define *patience* as tolerance. Patience does not mean to tolerate something. To be patient means to remain the same, to be consistent. Patience begins before the trouble, stays the same during the trouble, and is the same after the trouble has gone. In fact, the sameness is what brings you through the trouble.

You have to believe you are healed before sickness comes, when the symptoms show up, and then after they leave. That attitude of patience will bring a manifestation.

So patience is not sitting at the red light thinking, *Well, I just need to put up with the traffic.* No, you had joy before the traffic came. You have joy while you are in traffic. You will have joy when the traffic eases up. That is the biblical meaning of patience applied to real life.

EMPLOYING PATIENCE

Tribulation *worketh* patience. Tribulation does not produce or manufacture patience; it *works,* or *employs,* patience. In times of trouble we employ, or hire, patience. When we put patience to work in our lives, problems will not cause us to be shaken. Patience allows us to stand firmly on the truths we have learned from His Word. Our patience also *employs* the experience of victory.

I remain the same concerning the victory I know I am going to have as a result of my patience.

Finally, the experience *employs* hope, or an earnest expectation, and prepares you to receive from God. In other words, we know from experience that He will bring the victory; what He has done in the past has produced an expectation that since He did it before, He will do it now.

According to His Word, this is what we can expect while standing in righteousness and having access through our righteousness to the glory of God.

REDEEMED, RECONCILED, AND REMITTED

Previously, you read about Jesus' dying for us while we were ungodly, but look at this Scripture:

Much more then, being now justified by his blood, we shall be saved from wrath through him. For if, when we were enemies, we were reconciled to God by the death of his Son, much more, being reconciled, we shall be saved by his life. And not only so, but we also joy in God through our Lord Jesus Christ, by whom we have now received the atonement (Rom. 5:9-11).

Let me clarify this for those who say Christians must experience the seven-year tribulation when the Antichrist shows up. The Bible says we shall be saved from the wrath to come. (Rom. 5:10.)

"For if, when we were enemies, we were reconciled...." In this verse, the word "reconcile" in the original Greek is the verb *katallasso,* meaning "to change; to change from enmity to friendship."[1] So this verse would more accurately read, "For if, when we were enemies, we were [changed from enmity to friendship] to God by the death of his Son, much more, being [changed from enmity to friendship], we shall be saved by his life" (Rom. 5:10).

When we were enemies of God, we were changed from enmity to friendship with God through the blood of Jesus. We received Him, we were born again, and the righteousness of God came to live in our spirits.

THE REMITTING BLOOD

And not only so, but we also joy in God through our Lord Jesus Christ, by whom we have now received the atonement (Rom. 5:11).

The word *atone* means "to cover."[2] It seems as if the translators are saying that when we receive Jesus, we receive an atonement to cover our sins. However, the Greek word for "atonement" is the noun form of the Greek word used in verse 10 for "reconcile," *katallagh,* which actually means "to exchange."[3]

When we come to Jesus, we exchange our sins for God's righteousness. The sins are not covered but removed. We are washed in the blood and presented new and restored to the favor of God.

The blood of Jesus was not atoning blood. The blood of Jesus restored us to righteousness. The blood of Jesus did not cover your sin; it washed your sin completely away!

And not only so, but we also joy in God through our Lord Jesus Christ, by whom we have now received [the exchange] (Rom. 5:10).

We have received His righteousness in exchange for our sins through what Jesus did for us. If you missed the mark, in His righteousness you can be cleansed of that sin and continue unhindered. You have been totally changed from that life of sin to a life of righteousness.

As mentioned earlier, the apostle Paul was a Pharisee who spent several years methodically killing Christians, but in the righteousness of God he declared, "[I] have wronged no man..." (2 Cor. 7:2). He exchanged his past wrongs for the righteousness found in God.

Often, when you meet someone from your past who knew you before you knew Christ, they will begin talking about all of the things you used to do. But when you receive the righteousness of God, you can tell them that the person they are speaking of no longer exists. You can tell them that you are now the righteousness of God in Christ Jesus and you have made the exchange.

THE PROGRESSION

> Wherefore, as by one man [Adam] sin entered into the
> world, and death by sin; and so death passed upon all men,
> for that all have sinned (Rom. 5:12).

Do you see the progression? Adam disobeyed; sin came. With
sin came death and men died, spiritually and physically even if
they had not sinned.

Here is the significance of this:

> For until the law sin was in the world: but sin is not
> imputed when there is no law (Rom. 5:13).

How can sin be acknowledged when there is no law to break?
For example, you cannot go back to Abraham, Isaac, and Jacob
and say, "Look at all that sin in your life." You cannot acknowledge
anything they did wrong as *sin*. They could not be held accountable for sin, because there was no law.

They were sinners because of Adam's transgression, but there
must be a law to break for it to be wrong. They were not sinners
because they had broken a law; the law had not yet come. Man had
a sin nature because of what Adam did when Abraham and his
descendants were in his loins.

> Nevertheless death reigned from Adam to Moses, even
> over them that had not sinned after the similitude of
> Adam's transgression, who is the figure of him that was to
> come (Rom. 5:14).

Death was inevitable for everyone who was born, even those
who had never sinned after Adam. Sin was present in the earth
because it was committed through Adam.

How in the world could this sequence of events be unraveled? How could we possibly undo what has been done when we are the victims of it and have no power to affect it?

The answer was, and still is, Jesus.

> ...For if through the offence of one many be dead, much more the grace of God, and the gift by grace, which is by one man, Jesus Christ, hath abounded [multiplied and overflowed] unto many (Rom. 5:15).

Just as when Adam sinned and everybody in him was subject to the same punishment, Jesus came with the righteousness of God and all those in Him are the righteousness of God.

> And not as it was by one that sinned, so is the gift: for the judgment was by one to condemnation, but the free gift [righteousness] is of many offences unto justification [just as if you had never sinned]. For if by one man's [Adam's] offence death reigned by one; much more they which receive abundance of grace and the gift of righteousness shall reign in life by one, Jesus Christ (Rom. 5:16-17).

Those who receive righteousness shall rule in life by Jesus Christ. Are you ready to rule in life? You can when you stand in the righteousness of God. Now, do not interpret this to mean that it's okay to act arrogantly. That is not going to accomplish anything.

To rule in a situation is to be the determining voice. It means to be the one who determines the position, the outcome, and the result.

The ability to rule in the kingdom of God will frequently be accomplished not in disagreements, but in times of prayer.

You no longer have a license to sin. You have a license to practice the righteousness of God and be conformed to His righteousness.

> When we reign through righteousness, we will have the *zoe*, abundant, God-kind of eternal life, through Jesus Christ our Lord.

Moreover the law entered, that the offence might abound. But where sin abounded [overflowed and multiplied], [the grace of righteousness] did much more abound: that as sin hath reigned [ruled] unto death, [and nobody could do anything about it], even so might grace [rule] through righteousness unto eternal life... (Rom. 5:20-21).

It's important to understand that the eternal life mentioned in these verses is not referring to living forever. Remember when the rich young ruler came to Jesus and said, "Good Master, what good thing shall I do, that I may have eternal life?" (Matt. 19:16). He wasn't asking Jesus how to live forever. He was asking about zoe life; the God-kind of abundant life. In that passage, the Greek word for life is *zoe*.[4]

When we reign through righteousness, we will have the *zoe,* abundant, God-kind of eternal life, through Jesus Christ our Lord. (Rom. 5:21.)

That kind of life is what you have—a license to live, and to live abundantly. (John 10:10.)

A RIGHTEOUS
REBELLION

CHAPTER ELEVEN

So far, everything you have read up until now is in light of the righteousness of God. Now, this thought that we alluded to in the last chapter may come to you: *Now that I am in the righteousness of God, it seems as if I can do whatever I want to do because I have a right to miss the mark and be cleansed in His righteousness.*

The apostle Paul asked the same question this way, and then answered it.

What shall we say then? Shall we continue in sin, that [this] grace [of righteousness] may abound (Rom. 6:1)?

Does this mean we can sin and, when we are ready, return to the righteousness of God and be cleansed?

THE PRICE TAG FOR SIN

Before I answer that, let me share something that most preachers would never tell in fear that you would take advantage of it. Although you would sin repeatedly, if you confess your sin and ask forgiveness, God will honor His Word and cleanse you from all unrighteousness.

When you consider what you just read, though, remember that sin is a seed that has a harvest. God may be more forgiving and more merciful than the harvest of sin. You will indeed receive your forgiveness and cleansing, but you will also harvest your crop of the consequences of your sin, which has a very high price tag.

Let me give you an illustration. If you are a believer struggling in an area of sexual immorality, God will forgive you of your actions if you ask Him to. But His forgiveness will not stop the harvests of broken relationships, diminished self-worth, a wounded conscience, or sexually transmitted diseases in your life.

When these things happen, you are reaping a harvest that is making life more difficult for you. In the midst of this, God's attitude says, *I am not telling you not to sin because I have a problem with sin. I don't have a problem with sin, because My Son's blood took care of all that. I am telling you not to sin because every time you do, you sow a harvest that blocks My best from coming into your life. I love you, and I do not want the consequences of your sin to damage your faith or your ability to conform to My righteousness.*

So just as a man will not play with a lit stick of dynamite because of the danger it can cause, the Lord is saying that we should not play around with sin because of the terrible consequences it causes.

Take a look at your own life. Some of the things you are going through right now as a Christian are a result of not standing in your righteousness. It is time to take your stand and refuse sin no matter what. Why? Because you do not have a license to sin. You have a license to practice the righteousness of God.

AWAKEN TO RIGHTEOUSNESS

I've stopped eating for taste. I eat for nourishment. I discovered that I should eat this way and take care of myself because of the responsibility God has given me. I have a lot of work to do and it is going to take years to do it, so it's important to maintain my health. I must awaken to my righteousness, and sin not. (1 Cor. 15:34.)

I've also realized that as a parent, I am responsible for my children's health and their outcome. If I continue to go through the drive through and feed them junk food and they become sick one day, I cannot blame the devil by saying he attacked my children. No, they are just reaping a harvest of my actions. I cannot let that happen, because they are part of my assignment from the Lord.

> What shall we say then? Shall we continue in sin, that [the] grace [of righteousness] may abound? God forbid. How shall we, that are dead to sin, live any longer therein (Rom. 6:1-2)?

DEAD MAN SINNING

If we indeed are dead to our old sin nature, then it would be unnatural for us to sin now. Dead men do not sin. Reckon yourselves indeed to be dead to sin. (v. 11.)

Read through the following passage, and then we will pull it all together.

Know ye not, that so many of us as were baptized into Jesus Christ were baptized into his death? Therefore we are buried with him by baptism into death: that like as Christ was raised up from the dead by the glory of the Father, even so we also should walk in newness of life. For if we have been planted together in the likeness of his death, we shall be also in the likeness of his resurrection: knowing this, that our old man is crucified with him, that the body of sin might be destroyed, that henceforth we should not serve sin. For he that is dead is freed from sin.

Now if we be dead with Christ, we believe that we also shall live with him: knowing that Christ being raised from the dead dieth no more; death hath no more dominion over him. For in that he died, he died unto sin once: but in that he liveth, he liveth unto God.

Likewise reckon ye also yourselves to be dead unto sin, but alive unto God through Jesus Christ our Lord. Let not sin therefore [rule] in your mortal body, that ye should obey it in the lusts thereof. Neither yield ye your members as [weapons] of unrighteousness unto sin: but yield yourselves unto God, as those that are alive from the dead, and your members as instruments of righteousness unto God. For sin shall not have dominion over you: for ye are not under the law, but under grace (Rom. 6:3-14).

Paul is saying that because of Adam's betrayal, sin became dominate. But because of what Jesus did, sin no longer dominates. It no longer has dominion over your life. You do not have to sin if you do not want to sin, because it no longer dominates your nature.

This is a new day. This is a new way. You no longer *have* to sin. People sin because they want to, not because the devil makes them. It is time for you to rebel against the devil the same way you rebelled against God. Rebel against sin the same way you rebelled against God's righteousness. Be rebellious against the domain of darkness because it does not dominate you anymore, though it still wants to.

> The first lesson we have to learn to be free from the slavery of sin: we do not have to yield to it.

Understand something amazing. The sins you may be addicted to no longer dominate you as a born-again believer in the righteousness of God. Practice your rights and stop practicing your addiction.

Most members of Alcoholics Anonymous practice addiction during their AA meetings by confessing that they are alcoholics. They introduce themselves by saying, "Hello, my name is John Brown, and I am an alcoholic." Just once I would love for someone to introduce themselves by saying, "Hello, my name is John Brown, and I am the righteousness of God." God wants you to rebel against the sin that held you captive. It is no longer part of your identity.

WHOSE SERVANT AM I?

What then? shall we sin, because we are not under the law, but under grace? God forbid. Know ye not, that to whom ye yield yourselves servants to obey, his servants ye are to whom ye obey... (Rom. 6:15-16)?

Stop to consider whom you are obeying. Are you obeying the dictates of flesh unto sin or the prompting of the Spirit unto obedience, which will lead to righteousness?

The Bible says there are two masters—God and mammon (the world's system)—and you cannot love them both simultaneously. (Matt. 6:24.) When a test involving money comes, people are so quick to say, "Money is not *my* master." Then God says, *Give $1000,* and they say, "No." For that situation, money is their master.

"To whom ye yield yourselves servants to obey, his servants ye are...." Notice, yielding places the responsibility of movement on me. I yield; the devil does not push me into it. I yield thought by thought until I find myself doing something because I want to.

THE FIRST LESSON

The first lesson we have to learn to be free from the slavery of sin: we do not have to yield to it. However, when we do yield, we must recognize it is an act of our own will. If you curse at somebody who cut you off in traffic, the devil did not force you to do that. It is the act of yielding. You do it because you want to.

Although you may realize that you sinned as an act of your will, it is important to remember that you can also exercise your will not to sin.

You do not have to sin anymore, because you are the righteousness of God. Whatever sin it is, you do not have to continue in it any longer.

YIELDING TO RIGHTEOUSNESS IN HOLINESS

I speak after the manner of men because of the infirmity of your flesh: for as ye have yielded your members servants to uncleanness and to iniquity unto iniquity; even so now yield your members servants to righteousness unto holiness (Rom. 6:19).

Holiness is being of one mind with God. Whatever God thinks is right, you think is right. Whatever God thinks is wrong, you think is wrong. That is holiness.

When you are being tempted, rejoice because you have the ability to overcome it.

For when ye were the servants of sin, ye were free from righteousness. What fruit had ye then in those things whereof ye are now ashamed? for the end of those things is death.

But now being made free from sin, and become servants to God, ye have your fruit unto holiness, and the end everlasting life (Rom. 6:20-22).

Paul is expressing his concern about the fruit you bear. He is talking about sin.

For the wages of [payment for] sin is death; but the gift of God is [abundant, zoe (God-kind) of] eternal life through Jesus Christ our Lord [on this earth, as well as in heaven] (Rom. 6:23).

Paul is telling us how to avoid guilt and condemnation. Every time we sin, we will feel condemned, inadequate, and guilty. So why create a problem that will hold back the power of our righteousness?

THE PRESSURE OF TEMPTATION

This next Scripture is extremely encouraging.

> There hath no temptation taken you but such as is common to man... (1 Cor. 10:13).

Temptation is pressure applied to your flesh. Satan is like a pushy salesman who tries to pressure you into using his line of products called sin. However, you have not gone through anything that someone somewhere has not already experienced. That is because Satan has to use temptation that is common to man.

> ...but God is faithful, who will not suffer [allow] you to be tempted above that ye are able (to bear); but will with the temptation also make a way to escape, that ye may be able to bear it (1 Cor. 10:13).

God's commitment to you and to me is that He will not let the devil put pressure on our flesh, or tempt us beyond our ability to overcome that temptation. The temptations we face are according to our ability to overcome them. If you and I do not have the ability to overcome a certain temptation, God's commitment is that we will not be tempted in that area. So when you are being tempted, rejoice because you have the ability to overcome it.

You have everything it takes to overcome that temptation. You have everything it takes to remain in the righteousness of God;

otherwise, God Almighty would not have allowed temptation to come your way.

If you are being tempted, quit complaining, start rejoicing, and get out of that situation. God's Word says that *you are able to overcome.*

> ...no temptation or trial has come to you that is beyond human resistance and that is not adjusted and adapted and belonging to human experience, and such as man can bear]. But God is faithful [to His Word and to His compassionate nature], and He [can be trusted] not to let you be tempted and tried and assayed (or examined) beyond your ability and strength of resistance and power to endure, but with the temptation He will [always] also provide the way out (the means of escape to a landing place), that you may be capable and strong and powerful to bear up under it patiently (1 Cor. 10:13 AMP).

You have been guaranteed assistance from God Almighty: If temptation comes, God will assist you.

You are no longer a servant to sin. You are now the righteousness of God. You stand in your righteousness with heaven's support. You no longer have to allow the symptoms of sin to reign in your life. That means you can have victory 24 hours a day, seven days a week.

I encourage you to receive everything you have a right to as the righteousness of God. Speak it out of your mouth. Get confidence in it, and you will see you have been totally changed by the blood of Jesus!

STAY BALANCED

CHAPTER TWELVE

Until recently, I never realized how much God would do for those who believe and receive their righteousness. He said that there is much treasure in the houses of the righteous. (Prov. 15:6; Ps. 85:13.)

Beyond the reward promised to a righteous man, there is a temptation: The belief that those same good works can place you in right standing before God. In other words, many of us believe that our good works earn our righteousness. This is a general misunderstanding in the body of Christ that must be clarified.

This chapter addresses the issue of balance, or relationship, between good works and righteousness.

What shall we say then that Abraham our father, as pertaining to the flesh, hath found? For if Abraham were

139

justified by works, he hath whereof to glory; but not before God (Rom. 4:1-2.)

It is so easy to read that Scripture and think there is something wrong with good works. However, Paul is really saying that righteousnessis a gift. Good works will not earn it.

For what does the Scripture say? Abraham believed in (trusted in) God, and it was credited to his account as righteousness (right living and right standing with God). Now to a laborer, his wages are not counted as a favor or a gift... (Rom. 4:3-4 AMP).

When someone receives a paycheck, it is not a favor or a gift; instead it is something that the person has earned for the work they have done. Paul says a man's wages are owed to him.

Therefore, if a man were working to obtain his righteousness, then righteousness would not be a gift; it would actually be something owed to him. Many of us have done "good" things, with the thought that our efforts would somehow make us more righteous. It's time to change our thinking.

There is only one work that affects our righteousness: the work of salvation. This was accomplished through Jesus' sacrifice on the cross. Our faith in Him and His finished work (salvation) is what brings us into right standing with God. We must believe and receive the work of righteousness. We are recipients of a gift granted to us through His sacrifice and the shedding of His blood. Therefore, just like Abraham, we do nothing to be righteous. We simply believe God.

But to one who, not working [by the Law], (but who) trusts (believes fully) in Him Who justifies the ungodly, his faith is credited to him as righteousness (the standing acceptable to God) (Rom. 4:5 AMP).

> I must continue doing good works and be careful not to allow my belief in God's grace to cause me to quit working out my salvation.

But not as the offence, so also is the free gift. For if through the offence of one many be dead, much more the grace of God, and the gift by grace, which is by one man, Jesus Christ, hath abounded unto many. And not as it was by one that sinned, so is the gift: for the judgment was by one to condemnation, but the free gift is of many offences unto justification.

For if by one man's offence death reigned by one; much more they which receive abundance of grace and of the gift of righteousness shall reign in life by one, Jesus Christ. Therefore as by the offence of one judgment came upon all men to condemnation; even so by the righteousness of one the free gift came upon all men unto justification of life (Rom. 5:15-18).

Notice how many times the words "free gift" are used in this Scripture. Paul is emphasizing over and over that the only thing necessary for becoming righteous is faith. We cannot do anything to earn it or to make it happen.

OBTAINED BY FAITH

What shall we say then? That the Gentiles, which followed not after righteousness, have attained to righteousness, even the righteousness which is of faith. But Israel, which followed after the law of righteousness, hath not attained to the law of righteousness. Wherefore? Because they sought it not by faith... (Rom. 9:30-32).

Righteousness is activated by faith. When we operate in faith, we no longer walk by sight, or our feelings. (2 Cor. 5:7.) We lose our sin-consciousness and refuse to stand before God in inferiority, shame, or fear.

Not by works of righteousness which we have done, but according to his mercy he saved us, by the washing of regeneration, and renewing of the Holy Ghost; which he shed on us abundantly through Jesus Christ our Saviour; that being justified by his grace, we should be made heirs according to the hope of eternal life.

This is a faithful saying, and these things I will that thou affirm constantly, that they which have believed in God might be careful to maintain good works. These things are good and profitable unto men (Titus 3:5-8).

By demonstrating good works, you reveal God's goodness to others.

Although I am the righteousness of God, I must continue doing good works. I must also tithe, pray, attend church, and continue to be careful not to allow my belief in God's grace to cause me to quit working out my salvation. Remember, prayer does not make us righteous, but righteous people pray, which is a good work. Tithing does not make you righteous, but righteous people tithe, which is a good work. Attending church does not make you righteous, but righteous people do not forsake the gathering together of believers, which is another good work.

When you understand who you are in God and what your right standing with Him entitles you to, your level of confidence increases. This brings joy to God, but offense to those unfamiliar with the concept of righteousness. For example, many times an angry mob tried to kill Jesus because He declared Himself to be equal with God.

> Then the Jews took up stones again to stone him. Jesus answered them, Many good works have I shown you from my Father... (John 10:31-32).

It is important to understand the proper balance between good works and righteousness. It is also important to understand the importance of demonstrating good works in our everyday lives. Good works will *prove* your sonship.

> The Jews answered him, saying, For a good work we stone thee not; but for blasphemy; and because that thou, being a man, makest thyself God.

> Jesus answered them, Is it not written in your (own) law, (where) I said, Ye are gods?

> Say ye of him, whom the Father hath sanctified, and sent into the world, Thou blasphemest; because I said, I am the Son of God? If I do not the works of my Father, believe me not. But if I do, though ye believe not me,

believe the works: that ye may know, and believe, that the Father is in me, and I in him (John 10:33-34,36-38).

The good works we do are evidence of our righteousness. But the works do not *make* us righteous.

By demonstrating good works, you reveal God's goodness to others. It must be a conscious decision to love when you could hate, forgive when you have been deeply hurt, and give when it seems wiser to withhold. Those are the kinds of works that prove the righteousness of God in you.

Let your light so shine before men that they may see your moral excellence and your praiseworthy, noble, and good deeds and recognize and honor and praise and glorify your Father Who is in heaven (Matt. 5:16 AMP).

It is up to you to make sure that you are reflecting the image and the glory of God in this earth.

We cannot become religious with something as vital as the righteousness of God. Only evidence of good works will verify that you really stand for Him. Only good works will prove to a lost and dying world that you come from the Father, just as Jesus did.

In the past, religion has convinced many of us to put on a mask of piety so that we may be considered righteous. In this respect, good works were just a show that lacked integrity.

Several times over the years, I've had to examine myself. In many cases, I did not like what I saw, and I had to make changes.

I now realize that my life should prove that I am righteous. Without proof, it is all a religious mask.

We are the image and the glory of God. Yet we spend our lives searching for the glory instead of realizing we *are* the glory. What shines through determines God's reflection in us.

It is important to God that we reflect His character by imitating Him. (Eph. 5:1 AMP.) By nature we seek the supernatural. We want to see people in wheelchairs walk and blind eyes opened. But it is more important to me to please God and walk in love, honor, and integrity than to see many miracles in my ministry.

Children are a reflection of their parents. The same is true for us. We are a reflection of God, but what kind of reflection are we? Is the reflection the true image of God?

We must judge ourselves. Take a fresh look at yourself. You are the righteousness of God. It is up to you to make sure that you are reflecting the image and the glory of God in this earth.

> For we are God's [own] handiwork (His workmanship), recreated in Christ Jesus, [born anew] that we may do those good works which God prearranged (planned beforehand) for us certain paths to the good life. Many of us are currently walking those paths to a life of prosperity - spirit, soul and body. We're headed toward the good life where all of our needs are met; where we're out of debt and where we live in abundance (Eph. 2:10 AMP).

These good works are works of the power of God. These good works have burden-removing, yoke-destroying power because they flow out of a righteous believer. I believe God has prepared future paths for our lives.

In Genesis, Joseph took a path that was prepared for him ahead of time. I am certain that there were times when he questioned whether or not God was with him.

God prepared a future path for me. I once considered suicide. My life was a mess, and I often spent time questioning where God was and why He was allowing certain things to happen. But in time, I discovered that my path today is far better than the beginning.

Sometimes we become distracted and allow circumstances to throw us off course from God's divine plan for us. However, our decision as to whether or not we will fulfill God's will leads us to our destiny.

Who would have ever thought that being dropped in a pit, sold into slavery, thrown into jail, and being pushed around would lead Joseph to become the second most powerful man in Egypt? Yet, this was the path he had to travel in order to experience the good life.

STAY ON THE PATH

I believe God Almighty has predestined a path for you to take in your life because there is a good work awaiting you if you do not let fear take you out of God's will.

There were a number of obstacles I encountered on my way to where I am now. Often during my travels I was broke, but God predestined good works for me.

...[taking paths which He prepared ahead of time], that we should walk in them [living the good life which He prearranged and made ready for us to live] (Eph. 2:10 AMP).

His will is the good life. God knows what He is doing. You have to trust that.

We should strive to do the absolute best and allow God to show us how to walk the path He has prepared for us.

The following Scripture provides an example of instruction for a righteous man to do good works.

Charge them that are rich in this world, that they be not highminded, nor trust in uncertain riches, but in the living God, who giveth us richly all things to enjoy; that they do good, that they be rich in good works, ready to distribute, willing to communicate; laying up in store for themselves a good foundation against the time to come, that they may lay hold on eternal life (1 Tim. 6:17-19).

Paul gave us some illustrations in which he said to be rich in good works and ready to distribute. He also told us to be willing to communicate and to lay up in store a good foundation against the time to come, that we might lay hold on eternal life. (v. 19.) These are all good works. Some have used 1 Timothy 6:17 to justify living in lack and insufficiency. They overlook the

> Believers must be free from debt, lack, and insufficiency in order to do good to others as Jesus did while He was on earth.

entire verse, which goes on to say that God gives us all things richly to enjoy. Consequently, they are convinced that having riches leads to ungodliness. The Bible clearly says that fools are destroyed by prosperity. (Prov. 1:32.) A fool will squander wealth, whereas a wise man will use wealth for good works.

Paul is actually charging Timothy to warn those who are rich not to be foolish and high-minded with their wealth; that they should honor God with their finances by doing good works. Just as God is a giver, we must be givers as well.

Although I discuss financial prosperity in detail and how it relates to righteousness in Chapter 14, I feel the need to deal with this subject somewhat at this point.

Financial prosperity is essential in doing the work of Christ in these last days. It takes money to effectively evangelize the world. How can we spread the gospel through television, radio, books, and other means, if we lack the adequate finances to do so? We can't. Until the Body of Christ as a whole accepts this truth, we will never fully accomplish our mandate to "Go ye into all the world, and preach the gospel to every creature" (Mark 16:15).

For this reason, I have launched a "No More Debt" campaign. Believers must be free from debt, lack, and insufficiency in order to do good to others as Jesus did while He was on earth. Therefore, don't accept debt as a lifestyle; be free from it. Righteous people should know how to live debt-free and how to promote change in the lives of others word and deed.

Several years ago I began to question why people attend church. Why should I read the Bible? Why should I preach? My questions became a holy frustration. Then I asked God, "Why won't the preachers just open the Bible and simply explain what it means? Why won't they just preach it like a recipe book and tell me what to do?"

God answered me by saying "this is what you are called to do. You are called to bring understanding to the Body of Christ. There will be times when people will witness my power on your life and will say that your teachings make the Bible easier to understand".

My calling, my destiny in God, was a product of frustration. So if you are frustrated and cannot understand why something is not happening in the Body of Christ, it may be because God is calling *you* to do it.

WHAT IS IT ALL FOR?

Are you prepared for good works?

What do you do with this power? What do you do with this knowledge? What do you do with what you learn in Bible study? Does it stay in a notebook that goes in the trunk of your car until the next service?

How many lives have been changed because of your witness? When was the last time you led somebody to the Lord? Are you just enjoying the revelation, like a big Sunday dinner, without any exercise (good works)?

Believe it or not, good works are part of God's plan to bring others into right relationship with God. God is not willing that any should perish. (2 Peter 3:9.)

All scripture is given by inspiration of God, and is profitable for doctrine, for reproof, for correction, for instruction in righteousness (2 Tim. 3:16).

So what is the purpose of all this Scripture?

So that the man of God may be complete and proficient, well fitted and thoroughly equipped for every good work (2 Tim. 3:17 AMP).

It's for every good work.

How many lives have been changed because of your witness?

You have to allow a holy frustration to rise up on the inside of you that will compel you to do more—not because you are *trying* to be righteous, but because you *are* righteous. You can positively impact someone's world. You can positively impact your neighborhood. You can impact your family. You are the righteousness of God.

Good works are your testimony.

CONFIDENT
IN CHRIST

CHAPTER THIRTEEN

Confidence in God and in His Word is vital where our righteousness is concerned. In fact, an anointing is released in the lives of those who walk with confidence in their righteousness.

Satan wants to destroy your confidence in the Word of God and your righteousness. Let's examine what the Word of God has to say about confidence.

> For I am not ashamed of the gospel of Christ: for it is the power of God unto salvation to every one that believeth; to the Jew first, and also to the Greek. For therein is the righteousness of God revealed from faith to faith: as it is written, The just shall live by faith (Rom. 1:16-17).

Paul says that he is not ashamed of the good news of Jesus' ability to remove burdens and destroy yokes. This gospel is the power of God to everyone who believes it.

> For in the Gospel a righteousness which God ascribes is revealed, both springing from faith and leading to faith [disclosed through the way of faith that arouses to more faith]. As it is written, The man who through faith is just and upright shall live and shall live by faith (Rom. 1:17 AMP).

The power of God comes from the righteousness that is born out of faith in the Word but leads you right back to more faith in the Word.

Once you realize you are the righteousness of God, you should begin to do what the Word of God instructs so that you see more clearly God's predestined purpose for your life.

> And now, little children, abide in him; that, when he shall appear, we may have confidence, and not be ashamed before him at his coming. If ye know that he is righteous, ye know that every one that doeth righteousness is born of him (1 John 2:28-29).

When you begin to do the Word of God, you are operating by faith. Those who have been declared righteous live by faith. Therefore, confidence in your righteousness gives you the strength not to sin.

> Awake to righteousness, and sin not; for some have not the knowledge of God: I speak this to your shame (1 Cor. 15:34).

You may be thinking, *God has already taken care of our sin,* and He has. The blood of Jesus *has* cleansed you of your sin. *So why does the issue of sin keep coming up in John's letters?*

Righteousness should not mix with sin because it damages your confidence. When confidence is damaged, it is no longer effective and is eventually destroyed.

Sin attacks confidence. Think about it. You may have the confidence to pray and get answers to your prayers. You may have confidence that it is God's will to remove sickness from your body. You may have an unshakable faith in most things. But if you give in to temptation, guilt and condemnation will follow. Righteousness says that you can stand before God without guilt or condemnation. There is no condemnation to those who are in Christ. (Rom. 8:1.) However, sin attacks your right standing and erodes your confidence in the Word.

There is a way out. You have an Advocate (Jesus) with the Father.

> ...But if anyone should sin, we have an Advocate (One Who will intercede for us) with the Father - [it is] Jesus Christ [the all] righteous [upright, just, Who conforms to the Father's will in every purpose, thought, and action] (1 John 2:1 AMP).

The blood of Jesus cleanses you from sin. You can be forgiven and cleansed and still be the righteousness of God.

Why is confidence so important? Confidence is trust or reliance in something or someone. When you have confidence, yielding to temptation is not a problem; in fact, it's not even a concern. Confidence encourages you to yield to the Word of God and the anointing, rather than sin.

There were times in the early days of my ministry when miracles didn't happen the way they do now. The reason for this was not God's reluctance to perform them through me; it was because of my unwillingness to yield myself fully to Him. I did not really trust Him; I wasn't really sure about it. I thought that the church service could get completely out of control if I yielded completely. I was not prepared to take that chance.

The devil wants to destroy the confidence you have in God. He wants to keep you from trusting God and fulfilling His purpose. He knows there is something about confidence that produces power—even in the natural.

If you can tap into that place of trust and reliance, and your confidence level begins to rise, you will be a different person. When you pray in confidence, things will begin to happen that did not occur when you were unsure.

Cast not away therefore your confidence, which hath great recompence of reward (Heb. 10:35).

When you pray in confidence, things will begin to happen that did not occur when you were unsure.

We must not ever underestimate the value and importance of maintaining confidence in God and His Word. Confidence keeps us focused on God's will for our lives. This is not only a spiritual principle, but a natural one as well.

For example, let's say a person is learning to play basketball. He repeatedly shoots and misses. No matter how hard he tries he keeps missing the mark. Eventually he might quit and never play basketball again.

Or, he can have the confidence to keep trying. There is a learning process that he must be willing to go through; otherwise, he will become discouraged and begin to doubt that he will ever be a good basketball player. He could be one more shot away from a three-point basket or a rebound. If he holds on to the confidence that he can become good at basketball, he will improve his skills.

Unfortunately, most Christians quit before they see success. They grow weary and begin to doubt God.

Think for a moment about the areas in your life where you have cast away your confidence. What happened? You got stuck. You could not go any further. You created a roadblock of failure in your mind.

Now think about the times you told yourself that nothing would stop you from accomplishing your goal. It may have taken a while, but it is likely that you eventually achieved some measure of success.

Every righteous man or woman of God should possess confidence. It is not arrogance, but self-assuredness designed to keep you moving forward and the devil in his place. Confidence overcomes what the enemy says about you and reinforces what God says about you.

Confidence overcomes fear. When you are confident, you are fearless. You expect to see results.

Whenever our hearts in [tormenting] self-accusation make us feel guilty and condemn us. [For we are in God's hands.] For He is above and greater than our consciences (our hearts), and He knows (perceives and understands) everything [nothing is hidden from Him]. And, beloved, if our consciences (our hearts) do not accuse us [if they do not make us feel guilty and condemn us], we have confidence (complete assurance and boldness) before God, *and* we receive from Him whatever we ask, because we [watchfully] obey His orders [observe His suggestions and injunctions, follow His plan for us] and [habitually] practice what is pleasing to Him (1 John 3:20-22 AMP).

The condemnation, self-accusation, and guilt that come from sin are the enemies of confidence. By learning to govern your life away from sin, you will always have complete confidence before God.

How can you tell you are about to sin? Simple. Ask yourself if there is anything profitable about what you plan to do. If your heart is condemning you even a little, stop what you are doing.

The next time you are confronted with a temptation to sin, think about how sin affects your confidence. God wants your confidence at high levels so that you will not have to convince yourself that you are able to do what you do. You will simply *know* that you are able to complete a task.

This revelation hit me years ago when I wrote a book titled *Confidence: The Missing Substance to Faith.* I realized Christians are not very confident people. We talk the talk, but when it is time to produce results, we get scared. We do not have confidence. For example, we agree with the Word, but when God speaks to us and says, *All right, lay hands on this person,* we run for the pastor.

Where is our confidence?

Above average Christians are the ones who demand that their confidence extend to new levels. When such people stand in faith believing and operating in God's Word, the power of God is released.

> And this is the confidence that we have in him, that, if we ask any thing according to his will, he heareth us. And if we know that he hear us, whatsoever we ask, we know that we have the petitions that we desired of him (1 John 5:14-15).

Above average Christians are the ones who demand that their confidence extend to new levels.

There is something convincing about people who are quiet when facing challenges. They know what God has promised. They also know where they stand with God. (Isa. 30:15.)

Be wary of the ones who talk a lot. Most of the time they are trying to talk themselves and everyone else into something. They don't have any confidence.

When you have confidence in who you are, you don't have to talk a lot. All you have to do is keep a quiet resolve concerning who you are in Christ.

Here is the challenge to the believer: You have to make sure your confidence is in the Lord. You cannot put your confidence in man, because you will always be disappointed. You must make God the focus of your confidence, because he will never let you down. He is a sure foundation and a solid rock. He is the same yesterday, today, and forever. (Heb. 13:8.)

You and I should have no problem looking Jesus in the eye when He returns because of our confidence in Him. This requires a decision. Will you now focus on building up your confidence? Will you say no to sin?

Say this out loud: *In the name of Jesus, I declare victory over sin. I choose to awake to righteousness, and refrain from sin. In the name of Jesus, I will not cast away my confidence. I declare that I have a world-overcoming spirit, and I can do everything the Bible says I can do. I have what the Bible says I can have! I declare now before heaven and hell that I walk by faith and not by sight. I am not ashamed of the gospel of Christ, for it is the power of God unto salvation. I believe it. I receive it. I will not be shaken. I will not be moved. I am the righteousness of God in Christ Jesus. I have said it. It is so.*

YOUR RIGHT TO GOD'S BLESSINGS

CHAPTER FOURTEEN

It was my teaching on finances that led me to the study of righteousness. It seemed that in spite of all my teaching about prosperity and living debt-free, there were those who studied that teaching and were still buried by debt, suffering shortage, and living from paycheck to paycheck. The Spirit of God spoke to me to begin to teach on the righteousness of God so men and women in the Body of Christ could come to understand that they have a right to operate in the abundant life.

When sin entered the earth, so did death. Death came by sin, along with poverty, sickness, and lack. For us to walk free from all of that, we must understand that since the price has already been paid for our sin, we do not have to continue to live in the insanity of lack. We are redeemed from sin which includes poverty, sickness, and lack.

Something begins to happen in the lives of people when they realize that the blood of Jesus has delivered them from burdens and the good life awaits them.

For we are God's [own] handiwork (His workmanship), recreated in Christ Jesus, [born anew] that we may do those good works which God predestined (planned beforehand) for us [taking paths which He prepared ahead of time], that we should walk in them [living the good life which He prearranged and made ready for us to live] (Eph. 2:10 AMP).

God has prescribed for us to live the good life, so why aren't more people living it? First, it's because they do not think they have a legitimate right to prosper. Second, it's because their religious tradition has elevated life experiences over the Word of God and convinced them otherwise.

In this chapter, my objective is to show you that you have a right to prosper.

First, let's lay a scriptural foundation.

All scripture is given by inspiration of God, and is profitable for doctrine, for reproof, for correction, for instruction in righteousness: That the man of God may be perfect, thoroughly furnished unto all good works (2 Tim. 3:16-17).

160

Teaching prosperity makes many people uncomfortable, although it is in the Bible. I teach prosperity because it is God's will that we prosper in every area of our lives. (3 John 2.)

If prosperity did not appear in the Bible, then I would never deal with the subject. But since it is there, how can I continue to ignore Scriptures that deal with prosperity?

Second Timothy 3:16 says that all the Scriptures, are given by inspiration of God. Even the prosperity Scriptures are profitable for doctrine, for reproof, for correction, for instruction in righteousness.

The next verse tells us that these Scriptures are given to us, "That the man of God may be perfect (complete or mature), thoroughly furnished unto all good works" (v. 17).

You know, there are some good works God calls us to that we are not adequately furnished to carry out. By that I mean we lack the financial provision needed to fulfill the assignment He has given us. Second Timothy tells us that the Scriptures on prosperity exist so that we can be thoroughly furnished to *all* good works.

Scripture is the only thing profitable to correct the error of our thinking where prosperity is concerned. If I do not know what the Scriptures say, my efforts are not profitable.

If we are ever going to be mature Christians, proficient in prosperity, we cannot ignore the principles on prosperity found in God's Word. Paul says they were given so that the man of God could be "well fitted and thoroughly equipped for every good work" (v. 17 AMP). They are our benchmark, our standard of measurement.

People often say that because there are people around the world who need to hear about Jesus, there is no need to teach about prosperity as often as I do. But why would anyone want to hear about a Jesus who is broke and unable to lead them to a successful life? What would a person hope to attain in this life if nothing changes once they receive Jesus into their hearts? What is the point?

For whatsoever things were written aforetime were written for our learning, that we through patience and comfort of the scriptures might have hope (Rom. 15:4).

God is concerned about our success because we represent Him; we are ambassadors for Christ.

One of the most powerful things you can have is hope. Hope is that earnest expectation of something. It is the blueprint, the roadmap, which indicates your direction.

Hope has allowed my church to be what it is today. Hope is what brought you from where you used to be to where you are now. Without hope, people give up and become depressed and broken.

OLD AND NEW TOGETHER BY FAITH

Romans 15:4 says that the Old Testament Scriptures were "written for our learning" so that through them we might have hope. Now, you cannot believe the New Testament, without also believing the Old Testament. It is all the Word of God.

We know that everything God has for us in the Bible functions and operates by faith. Healing, deliverance, and prosperity are all received by faith.

So then faith cometh by hearing, and hearing by the
word of God (Rom. 10:17).

If God's Word says you are supposed to prosper and if faith
comes by hearing the Word (Rom. 10:17), then I will teach this
Word until people are convinced that they are destined to prosper.
I will teach these truths until they refuse to tolerate anything less
than the success and the prosperity God promises in His Word.

You do *not* have to compromise to succeed. You do *not* have to
cheat or operate unethically to succeed in life.

You have the Word of God. You have the name of Jesus. You
have the Holy Spirit, and God is well able to bring His Word to pass.

Words have meaning, but some words do not mean what we think
they mean. Through time, the meaning of the word *prosperity* has
changed. As people changed the way they used the word, its meaning
changed. Let's examine how its usage has changed over time.

When most people hear the word *prosperity,* their first thought
is money. But the subject of prosperity is not just about money, it's
about our whole lives.

For example, there is prosperity of the spirit. There is prosperity
of the soul. There is prosperity of the physical body. There is prosperity in marriage. And there is also prosperity in financial matters.

...Let the Lord be magnified, which hath pleasure in
the prosperity of his servant (Ps. 35:27).

What, exactly, is this prosperity that the Lord takes pleasure
in? The word "prosperity" is derived from the Hebrew word

shalom, which is where we get the English word *peace.* This Hebrew word *shalom,* means "well being, completeness, wholeness, nothing missing and nothing broken in your life."[1] In other words total life prosperity.

But in this Scripture it is translated "prosperity." The translator could just as easily have said, "Let the Lord be magnified, who has pleasure in your peace." Or "Let the Lord be magnified, who has pleasure in your well being." Or "Let the Lord be magnified, who has pleasure in your success in every area." Most of the time in the Old Testament when you see the word "prosperity," it is referring to a much higher level of success than just acquiring money. Psalm 35:27 tells us that God takes pleasure in this level of success among His servants.

Joshua 1:8 essentially says, "Meditate in the Word day and night, so that you will make your way prosperous and have good success."

God is concerned about our success because we represent Him; we are ambassadors for Christ. God wants His children to be as successful as He is. Success is the hope of every father who loves his child. God cannot make Jesus successful without also making the joint heirs of Jesus successful. But it does not happen automatically; it comes by faith.

We have come to realize that we are the righteousness of God. Therefore when we call Him Father, we understand that we are sons and heirs of God and joint heirs with Christ Jesus. (Rom. 8:17.)

God wants us to be successful in our physical bodies: healthy. He wants us to be successful in our spirits: born again. He wants us to be successful in our souls: possessing a sound mind. But for some reason, many of us keep running into this mental block when it comes to understanding financial success because we base our faith and expectations on our experience rather than on what God's Word says about it.

TRUE PROSPERITY

What is true prosperity? Here are several definitions. Prosperity is being in control of your circumstances and your situations. It also means meeting the needs of humankind regardless of what those needs may be. Prosperity means being successful in any endeavor in your life, or making good progress in the pursuit of anything desirable.

The key is that true prosperity will always extend beyond your needs. Until your prosperity not only satisfies you but also overflows into the lives of others, you are not biblically prosperous.

Let them shout for joy, and be glad, that favour my righteous cause: yea, let them say continually, Let the Lord be magnified, which hath pleasure in the prosperity of his servant. And my tongue shall speak of thy righteousness and of thy praise all the day long (Ps. 35:27-28).

Notice two things here. First, God has pleasure in your prosperity. Second, there is a connection between God's righteousness and His pleasure in your prosperity.

The world may not take pleasure in your prosperity, but God is pleased with it. Your family may not take pleasure in your prosperity, but God enjoys it thoroughly. There are even some preachers who have no pleasure in prosperity, but according to the Word, God has pleasure in our prosperity.

If God takes pleasure in my prosperity, then I want to have pleasure in it also. Holiness is agreeing with what God says and thinking the way He thinks. Therefore, if God takes pleasure in the prosperity of His servant, He certainly takes pleasure in the prosperity of His children. And as His sons and daughters we should enjoy it as well.

Now let's take a look at the key connection between our prosperity and God's righteousness.

...Let the Lord be magnified, which hath pleasure in the prosperity of his servant. And my tongue shall speak of thy righteousness all the day long (Ps. 35: 27-28).

Our prosperity is a reflection of God's righteousness in our lives.

Our prosperity is a reflection of God's righteousness in our lives. We should speak of our well being and wholeness, in all areas of our lives daily. Total life prosperity belongs to those who receive the righteousness of God and everything else that the blood of Jesus provides. The fact that someone has wealth is not proof that he is walking in God's righteousness.

Real prosperity is having the ability to choose to do what you want to do when you want to do it. You do not have to have lavish things in order to be prosperous. As a prosperous person, you are able to do what you want to do and not be limited or controlled by the world's system.

Think about having that kind of freedom of choice. That is exactly what God has been trying to protect. God made us men and women with the freedom to choose.

Because of lack, many of us cannot *afford* to obey God. When God moves on Your spirit and tells you to do something, Satan comes right behind that command and reminds you of how little you have so that you will fail to accomplish God's instruction. Because of this, many end up disobeying God because they are controlled by their lack of money.

Just because a person has material things does not mean he is in control. When you borrow money to buy a mansion, and borrow money to get a Rolls Royce, and borrow some more money to get furniture, you may end up with a load of stuff, but the real price tag is slavery to your creditors. Borrowing money to purchase material things is nothing but a license to pretend.

True prosperity is being able to control your circumstances and situations, while being unlimited by this world's system.

Material possessions that result in debt ultimately control you. That is not prosperity. Prosperity cannot be measured solely by the amount of substance a person possesses.

Consider this illustration. A couple of years ago I took my cousin to buy a car. He had just graduated from college and was working as a college coach. He was doing well, and the Lord spoke to me to buy him a car.

I let him pick out the car he wanted, and we sat down to fill out the paperwork. The first thing he asked was how we were going to work out the loan?

He obviously didn't know how I did business. So, I just told him to sit back and see what real prosperity is.

When you go to buy a house or a car and they know you need financing, you are under the creditor's control. They can dictate the terms of the sale. However, when you walk in there with your own money to make a purchase, you are in control of the situation. That is real prosperity.

The salesman came over to us, and I told him what car we planned to buy.

He was a little taken by surprise, but he recovered nicely and told us the price while pointing to the dealer sticker on the window.

I paused a moment to make sure neither he nor my cousin would miss my next statement.

I told him that I saw the price on the tag, but I would not pay that much for the car. So, I offered him the price I was willing to pay. I then took a check out and started to write. I showed the salesman the amount I had written on the check; then I waited a second or two and I told him that someone would get my business that day. It was his choice whether it would be him or another car dealership.

After I did that, he excused himself to go speak to his manager. But there was nothing his manager could do. Neither one of them had control of the situation. I did.

God wants that kind of control back into the hands of His people. He wants us to go into the world's financial system and let people know that we will not be controlled. True prosperity is being able to control your circumstances and situations, while being unlimited by this world's system. It is the ability to make an impact in someone's life and make a mark that cannot be erased.

MAKING GOD YOUR SOURCE

It's important to understand that when you make God your source, you no longer have to live by your paycheck. Your check becomes the seed you sow.

I finally understood this years ago, when my annual salary was $18,000. I realized that it was not enough money to live on, so I used my pay as a bag of seed. I told the Lord that whatever He told me to do, I would do, and whatever He told me to give, I would give. As I started doing that, I kept track of my giving in a ledger.

I saw God take the seed I planted and multiply it a hundred fold. For example, I would go and preach at another church, and the church would give me a speaking honorarium of $100,000— for just two days.

I would tithe on it and sow the rest in various places. Then I would go somewhere else to preach and someone would tell me that the Lord told them to give me a check—often in very large amounts.

Not all preachers prosper. Not even all preachers with big churches prosper. Only those who believe in the principle of prosperity, do the work, and sow the seeds, prosper.

We have to be careful how we determine prosperity. We use all the wrong measurements to determine prosperity. But your source is not your check; God is your Source. Your source is not your business; God is your Source.

You will know what it means to prosper by the Word of God once you allow God to be your Source.

God is my Source. Meditate on that until it becomes real in your mind and heart.

Page one in God's prosperity manual is realizing and verbalizing that God is your Source. You cannot go to page two until you are living page one. *God is my Source.* Meditate on that until it becomes real in your mind and heart. *God is my Source!*

THE LAW OF TRANSFORMATION

CHAPTER FIFTEEN

In the previous chapter, we learned that prosperity is the ability to be in control of your circumstances and situations. It is the ability to choose how you want to live.

That is just the beginning. If we stop there, we've only touched the surface of what true biblical prosperity really is. We have to go to the next step, which is having enough to be in control: taking care of all our needs and our desires, and then being able to impact the lives of others. Real prosperity always touches someone else's life.

Your faith has not reached its highest point as long as you are using it only for yourself.

It is the same where prayer is concerned. When you pray as the righteousness of God, God answers your prayers and you have confidence that He hears you; then you know that you have those things

> Real financial
> success has
> not reached its
> highest level
> until you can use
> your prosperity
> to impact someone
> else's life.

you have prayed for. Yes, it is working for you, but prayer is not at its highest point until you can use what you have learned about prayer to become effective in using it to impact someone else's life.

So it is with prosperity. It is not enough that you become financially prosperous and successful, able to do what you want to do, able to fulfill your dreams, and able to control your life and your situations. Real financial success has not reached its highest level until you can use your prosperity to impact someone else's life.

THE EVOLUTION OF "PROSPERITY"

Let's walk through the evolution of the word "prosperity," which in the Greek is *euodoo*.

Originally, *euodoo* was a parting utterance like "goodbye," "Godspeed," "bon voyage," or "farewell." The first part of the word means "good" or "well." The last part of the word means "a roadway, a trip, or travel."

Euodoo originally meant "to be on the right road; to grant an expeditious or an unhindered journey, or to successfully reach the destination safe and sound; to be led along a good road; being on a road that is easy to travel."[1]

The word "prosperity" *(euodoo)* is only used in the New Testament four times, but it evolves in three stages from the first time to the last.

Remember when "cool" used to refer to the temperature and a "dog" used to refer to man's best friend? Now each of these words is used to mean something different than before. Well, this same transformation of meaning is what happened with the word "prosperous."

Making request, if by any means now at length I might have a prosperous journey by the will of God to come unto you (Rom. 1:10).

Paul is speaking here of a successful journey.

But, if we look at 1 Corinthians 16, we begin to see evidence that the word "prosperity" has changed with usage. Now we see that the travel metaphor has evolved into a word for material or financial prosperity.

Now concerning the collection for the saints, as I have given order to the churches in Galatia, even so do ye. Upon the first day of the week let every one of you lay by him in store, as God hath prospered him, that there be no gatherings when I come (1 Cor. 16:1-2).

Here we see Paul encouraging the church at Corinth to give to the Lord as God has given to them. He is using the word "prospered" in the sense of material wealth, saying, "Lay aside as God has prospered you to lay aside." This does not refer to a successful journey. It is now referring to prosperity in material things.

Third John 2 shows further evolution of the words concerning prosperity. Now, instead of narrowing the meaning, John broadens it significantly.

Beloved, I wish above all things that thou mayest prosper and be in health, even as thy soul prospereth (3 John 2).

Here John is talking about your spiritual, physical, and financial prosperity. *Euodoo* in this sense means continuous well-being in every area of your life.[2]

Prosperity has now evolved from its original travel metaphor to one of total life prosperity.

FAITH VS. PRESUMPTION

There is a big difference between faith and presumption. Some members of the Body of Christ have been doing things and calling it faith, when it is not faith at all. It is presumption. Presumption is not faith. Often Christians are wasting their time with presumption and not faith.

You have to cultivate your faith through the Word of God to sustain your growth in the area of financial prosperity.

You choose presumption instead of faith if you write a check and put it into the offering when there is no money in your bank account to cover that check. You may believe that you are applying faith and sowing seed with the thought, *"God will send the money before that check gets deposited."* However this is not faith at all.

The presumption is that the act of writing the check will release something in the spiritual realm and money will come to you. The Bible does not tell us to do that.

Writing checks will not make you a millionaire. You have to cultivate your faith through the Word of God to sustain your growth in the area of financial prosperity.

What you *can* do is write the check and leave it in your desk drawer and use it as a point of contact to release your faith for what you believe God will do while you declare His promises. *That* is faith.

THE SURE REWARD

The wicked worketh a deceitful work: but to him that soweth righteousness shall be a sure reward. As righteousness tendeth to life: so he that pursueth evil pursueth it to his own death (Prov. 11:18-19).

Now consider the meaning of "reward." A reward is something you get as a result of something extra you did. For example, your paycheck would not be a reward, but a bonus would be.

I want to show you that prosperity is a reward.

Can you see God coming down after you've lived a great life and saying, "Behold, I grant unto you poverty. Be in lack all the days of your life"? Nobody is going to get excited over that. Prosperity is a reward.

Blessed is the man that walketh not in the counsel of the ungodly, nor standeth in the way of the sinners, nor sitteth in the seat of the scornful. But his delight is in the law of the Lord; and in his law doth he meditate day and night. And he shall be like a tree planted by the rivers of water, that bringeth forth his fruit in his season; his leaf also shall not wither; and whatsoever he doeth shall prosper (Ps. 1:1-3).

Now, if you avoid the counsel of the ungodly, don't associate with sinners, don't sit with the scornful; if you meditate on God's Word day and night, look at the reward God promises—*whatsoever you do will prosper.*

God says that if you do these things, your reward is prosperity. It is not going to come because you are doing the minimum requirements. It is going to come as a result of you going beyond the call of duty.

Only be thou strong and very courageous, that thou mayest observe to do according to all the law, which Moses my servant commanded thee: turn not from it to the right hand or to the left, that thou mayest prosper whithersoever thou goest (Josh. 1:7).

Now, this word "prosper" in verse 7 comes from the Hebrew word *sakal,* which means, "to do wisely."[3] So we can also read it to say, "That thou mayest [do wisely] whithersoever thou goest."

This book of the law shall not depart out of thy mouth; but thou shalt meditate therein day and night, that thou mayest observe to do according to all that is written therein: for then thou shalt make thy way prosperous, and then thou shalt have good success (Josh. 1:8).

If you do these things, the reward is prosperity.

Deuteronomy 8:1 says, "All the commandments which I command thee this day shall ye observe to do, that ye may live, and multiply, and go in and possess the land which the Lord sware unto your fathers."

Did Jesus do what God told Him to do? Of course He did. As a result, Jesus was not poor. If He had been, it would have been a violation of spiritual and scriptural principle. There is no way you can do God's Word, keep His commandments, walk in His ways, and be denied prosperity. It just will not happen.

God's promise of prosperity works in every country, in every neighborhood, and in every person. The reward comes if you do what you are supposed to do.

> **There is no way you can do God's Word, keep His commandments, walk in His ways, and be denied prosperity.**

Here is an example of this principle working in the lives of four men: sixteen-year-old King Uzziah, Solomon, David, and Hezekiah.

> Then all the people of Judah took Uzziah, who was sixteen years old, and made him king....
>
> Sixteen years old was Uzziah when he began to reign, and he reigned fifty and two years in Jerusalem....
>
> And he sought God in the days of Zechariah, who had understanding in the visions of God: and as long as he sought the Lord, God made him to prosper (2 Chronicles 26:1,3,5).

The reward to King Uzziah for seeking the Lord was prosperity.

Now, my son, the Lord be with thee; and prosper thou, and build the house of the Lord thy God… (1 Chron. 22:11).

David is speaking to his son Solomon. Solomon is going to need money if he is going to build a house for God.

Only the Lord give thee wisdom and understanding, and give thee charge concerning Israel, that thou mayest keep the law of the Lord thy God (1 Chron. 22:12).

Do you know that wisdom and understanding can promote your prosperity?

Then shalt thou prosper, if thou takest heed to fulfil the statutes and judgments which the Lord charged Moses with concerning Israel: be strong, and of good courage; dread not, nor be dismayed (1 Chron. 22:13).

He says, if you do these things, you will prosper.

Now it came to pass in the third year of Hoshea son of Elah king of Israel, that Hezekiah the son of Ahaz king of Judah began to reign.

And he did that which was right in the sight of the Lord....

He trusted in the Lord God of Israel; so that after him was none like him among all the kings.... For he clave to the Lord, and departed not from following him, but kept his commandments, which the Lord commanded Moses.

And the Lord was with him; and he prospered whithersoever he went forth: and he rebelled against the king of Assyria, and served him not (2 Kings 18:1,3,5-7).

This is a reward to Hezekiah. Scripture says there was no other king like Hezekiah because he kept God's commandments, walked in His statutes, and kept His ways.

GOD IS A REWARDER

God wants you to be successful. If you are not successful, examine your life. Study the statutes of God. When you really get to know the statutes of God, you will be able to keep them and experience the reward of prosperity.

But without faith it is impossible to please him: for he that cometh to God must believe that he is, and that he is a rewarder of them that diligently seek him (Heb. 11:6).

How do you receive the reward of prosperity? By steadily *seeking Him,* not just on Sunday, but every day. Prosperity is a sure reward for those who steadily and diligently seek God. Seek His ways, obey His Word and do what He tells you to do without compromise.

Beloved, I pray that you may prosper in every way and [that your body] may keep well, even as [I know] your soul keeps well and prospers (3 John 2 AMP).

Here is the reward God wants to give us: that we should prosper in every way—in our bodies, souls, finances, and other ways as well.

THE LAW OF TRANSFORMATION

If you are thinking, *This all sounds good, but I don't think it would ever work for me,* then let me show you the key that can change your life forever.

In order to advance to full, rich, overflowing total life prosperity, you have to change. You have to be transformed. If you keep doing the same thing, you are only going to maintain what you have right now.

Insanity is when a man continues to do the same thing and expects different results.

The law of transformation is addressed in the book of John:

> And the third day there was a marriage in Cana of
> Galilee; and the mother of Jesus was there: and both Jesus
> was called, and his disciples, to the marriage. And when
> they wanted wine... (John 2:1-3).

> ...the mother of Jesus saith unto him, They have no wine.

> Jesus saith unto her, Woman, what have I to do with thee? mine hour is not yet come.

> His mother saith unto the servants, Whatsoever he saith unto you, do it (John 2:3-5).

Insanity is when a man continues to do the same thing and expects different results.

Here is the principle of transformation, the principle for change: *Whatsoever He saith unto you, do it.* Obedience is the key to transformation. Without fail, you will change if you are willing to do what God says to do.

The first thing God said to do was to fill the pots with water. (v. 7.) This is symbolic. If you want change, the first thing you have to do is fill your spirit with the water of God's Word. If you want prosperity, you have to get filled up to the top with the Word on prosperity. You must meditate in it and study it for yourself.

Set aside an hour a day with your Bible and study it for yourself. Learn how to use study materials, such as concordances, dictionaries, and study Bibles.

The impact on your life will be great when you develop a personal relationship with God. The reason there is so much confusion in the Body of Christ right now is that instead of saying what God says in His Word, many people rely solely upon what the preacher says. Nothing the preacher says will do you any good if it does not come from the Word.

Fill yourself up with the water of God's Word; and whatever He tells you to do, do it.

If you want your water to turn to wine, and you believe that all good and perfect gifts come from Him, you have to make the decision to do everything God tells you to do. Create a checklist for yourself:

Am I obeying God?

Am I doing what God told me to do?

Am I treating people right?

Am I walking in love?

Am I walking in forgiveness?

Lord, what is stopping my prosperity?

Am I walking in covetousness?

Am I walking in strife?

Am I a busybody?

Whatever He says to you, do it.

THE TRANSACTION OF OBEDIENCE

I just cannot afford to disobey God because there is still much transformation needed to get me to the "level" of anointing where I can do exactly what I was born to do.

Doing what God says to do is the master key to transformation from shortage to abundance, from poverty to prosperity. Follow the leading of the Holy Spirit. It is the transaction of obedience.

There is no reason why we should be "in the dark" about what our righteousness entitles us to.

Doing what God tells you to do where your marriage is concerned. Doing what God tells you to do where your children are concerned. Doing what God tells you to do where your job is concerned. Doing what God tells you to do where your money is concerned.

THE PRINCIPAL THING

The Bible says, "Wisdom is the principal thing..." (Prov. 4:7). The Scriptures tell us, "Counsel in the heart of man is like deep water; but a man of understanding will draw it out" (Prov. 20:5).

How do you draw wisdom out? By praying in the Holy Spirit. (1 Cor. 2:7,10-14; 14:2.) Praying in the Holy Spirit is the same as praying in tongues. Wisdom abides right on the inside of you. When you pray in the Holy Spirit, you're pulling wisdom out. It does not abide in your brain; it abides in your spirit.

When you pray in the Holy Spirit, you are saying you believe that you receive God's wisdom by faith. You may not know what you are saying; but you know it is God's will because Romans 8:26-27 says that the Holy Spirit helps us to pray according to His will. *The Amplified Bible* says, "... the Spirit intercedes and pleads [before God] in behalf of the saints according to and in harmony with God's will" (v. 27). In simple terms, when we pray in tongues, the Holy Spirit prays with and through us when we don't know what to pray for in our natural thinking. He does so in line with God's will.

I like what 1 Corinthians 14:2, in *The Amplified Bible* says "... one who speaks in an [unknown] tongue speaks not to men but to God, for no man understand or catches his meaning, because in the [Holy] Spirit he utters secret truths and hidden things [not obvious to the understanding]."

Deuteronomy 29:29 says that the secret things that belong to God, belong to us as well. The Holy Spirit's job includes revealing to us the mystery and reality of our sonship. (1 Cor. 2:9-10.) This tells me that there is no reason why we should be "in the dark" about what our righteousness entitles us to.

Although the things we need answers to may be hidden from our natural understanding, they are revealed to our human, reborn spirit. "For what person perceives (knows and understands) what passes through a man's thoughts except the man's own spirit within him? Just so no one discerns (comes to know and comprehend) the thoughts of God except the Spirit of God" (v. 11 AMP).

I believe Jesus was referring to speaking in tongues when He said, "… out of (your) belly shall flow rivers of living water" (John 7:38). In this Scripture, the belly represents your spirit. The rivers of living waters represent wisdom, understanding, and hidden secrets revealed by the Holy Spirit. Now you can understand the importance of praying in tongues.

Certain things may be a mystery or secret to you—getting out of debt, restoring your marriage, or getting healed. They don't have to be. Tap into the wisdom of God and begin experiencing the full benefits of your sonship with God.

If you are not Spirit-filled with the evidence of speaking in tongues, make it a priority. I can think of no better place to start in your quest to hear the voice of the Holy Spirit.

He says you speak hidden secrets, wisdom that is hidden from your brain but is in the Holy Spirit. When you pray in the spirit, you are speaking secrets or, as the Bible calls them, mysteries.

When you pray in the Spirit, you are pulling the wisdom up from your spirit by the Holy Spirit. By doing so you release your faith and receive God's instruction through the Holy Spirit.

For the most part when you finish praying in the Spirit, nothing will have hit your conscious mind.

But if you stay in faith, there is always what the Bible calls a due season. (Gal. 6:9.) There is a due season when all the wisdom you have been pulling up, and all the faith you've been releasing is going to be made plain to your understanding.

It could be that all of a sudden some good idea will strike your mind, and you will understand something in an instant and with a depth and clarity beyond ordinary wisdom. Then you will realize there was no way in the world you could have come up with that idea on your own; it had to be God.

And before you know it, a million-dollar corporation is given birth by the wisdom of God.

I am telling you, that is how it happens.

The devil has fought praying in the Spirit for so long because it is the bucket you use to dip into the wellspring of God's wisdom for your life, your job, your relationships, and your ministry.

Start calling those things that be not as though they were, and start praying in the Holy Spirit every day. Believe that you receive the things you desire to come to pass, and God will show you exactly what needs to be done. When that happens, make sure you write it down because God is about to transform you from average to superabundance.

Your reward will be prosperity.

THE GREAT EXCHANGE

Divine fellowship with God and the righteousness of God go together. Fellowship with God and with each other should be a distinguishable mark of every Christian. (1 John 1:7.) When you spend time with God in the Word, in prayer, and in the area of obedience, people should be able to look at you and realize that you spend time with the Father.

That word *fellowship* also means "a mutual sharing or exchange."[1] In other words, when you spend time with God in fellowship, an exchange will take place. You exchange your weaknesses for His strengths and His revelation.

Married people should desire to spend time with their spouses. That should be a distinguishing mark of someone who is married. In the course of their fellowship, married couples exchange ideas, make plans, and set strategies for their lives together. The result of their fellowship is love. They grow closer and more in love with each other and the cycle of exchange through fellowship is repeated.

The same is true with our fellowship with the Father. Spending time in the Word and in prayer brings a divine exchange, and the result is love for Him. Your fellowship with God will cause your love for Him to increase.

When love is born out of that fellowship time, you will give birth to confidence. Because you spend time with God and you love Him, you are now confident that He will do what He tells you He will do.

Even if you don't know much about the Bible or prayer, your time with God is never wasted. The fact is, the more time you spend with Him, the more time you will want with Him. He creates the hunger that He alone can satisfy.

You might know every Scripture, but not know Jesus. The more time you spend with the Father, the better you will know Him. The more time you spend with Him, the less convinced you will be that He is alright with you being broke and in debt. Get to know Him better. He is a Father. And would any father want to keep his child down?

> Because you spend time with God and you love Him, you are now confident that He will do what He tells you He will do.

If you spend time with Him, it will also birth an assurance on the inside of you. You will be convinced of His goodness, as well as your righteousness. That is what many of us lack. We have a lot of doctrine but no assurance, or belief in that doctrine. And you will not be assured of your righteousness until you spend time with the Father.

The time you spend abiding with the Father will enhance your life in His righteousness. When you abide with Him, you are convinced you have rights as His child. You are not going to accept any less than what is rightfully yours.

This conviction now begins to lead you into the study of the Word to find evidence of what you know. Your assurance should lead your research, not vice-versa.

I want to know the Father. I want to know the Word too, because you cannot separate them. When you know the Word, you know the Father. Similarly, when you have spent time in fellowship with the Father, His Word will become that much more alive to you. Know the Father: know the Word. Know the Word: know the Father.

> Abide in me, and I in you. As the branch cannot bear fruit of itself, except it abide in the vine; no more can ye, except ye abide in me. I am the vine, ye are the branches: He that abideth in me, and I in him, the same bringeth forth much fruit: for without me ye can do nothing. If a man abide not in me, he is cast forth as a branch, and is withered; and men gather them, and cast them into the fire, and they are burned. If ye abide in me, and my words abide in you, ye shall ask what ye will, and it shall be done unto you (John 15:4-7).

This word "abide" means "to rest; to dwell." It also means "to continue permanently or in the same state."[2] This gives you the picture of something being firm and immovable, something that remains and continues or resides and rests. There is a sense of continuity that comes from this word "abide." When we abide, we are not only dwelling, but we continue to dwell. We are not just remaining; we continue to remain. We are not just resting; we continue to rest.

This is what our walk with God will have to look like in order for the effect of our righteousness to manifest in our lives: abiding continuously, resting continuously, dwelling continuously in His Word and in His presence—in Him.

> Abide in me, and I in you. As the branch cannot bear
> fruit in itself, except it abide in the vine... (John 15:4).

Jesus is saying here that we should set up residence and remain in Him continuously.

> **If God is truly not doing anything in your life, it is because you are not inviting Him into your life.**

If you break a branch of an apple tree, will that branch be able to produce any more apples? No. Only as long as that branch is on that tree can it produce apples. That is exactly what Jesus is saying. As long as we are in Him, we can do anything.

I thought about this phrase "in Him" recently. Every time I say "in Him" I see myself standing in a big pot, and as long as I stay in that pot I can do anything He can do. But as soon as I step out of that pot, I realize that I am attempting to do things within my human ability instead of trying to do things in His ability.

If you stay in Him, it will be difficult for you to sin. It is when you step out of Him that you are going to do things that are opposite to His will.

You cannot bear any fruit unless you abide in the vine. Jesus made that clear. It should not be a big surprise if we do not bear fruit and do not see results. It should not be a big surprise if we do not see love, faith, longsuffering, and the fruit of the Spirit in our lives if we are not in Him.

> I am the vine, ye are the branches: He that abideth in me, and I in him, the same bringeth forth much fruit: for without me ye can do nothing (John 15:5-7).

Here it is again.

> If a man abide not in me, he is cast forth as a branch, and is withered; and men gather them, and cast them into the fire, and they are burned. If ye abide in me, and my words abide in you, ye shall ask what ye will, and it shall be done unto you.

> If ye keep my commandments, ye shall abide in my love (John 15:6-7,10).

I can picture the Father manifesting Himself and calling it His love. The things your father will do for you, the things you do as a parent, are manifestations of love. And that is what Jesus is saying here. You can live on in His love if you continue to abide in Him.

The problem is not that God does not want to do anything in your life. If God is truly not doing anything in your life, it is because you are not inviting Him into your life. You have to decide who you are and what you are going to do. It is time to abide *continuously*.

> He that saith he abideth in him ought himself also so
> to walk, even as he walked (1 John 2:6).

If I say I abide in Him, in light of my righteousness, I have a right to do just what He does. As the righteousness of God, I can do all that Jesus can do because I am doing it in Him—not in my flesh.

If you say you abide in Him, then you ought to walk like Him because of the faith in your righteousness and the conviction that you abide in Him. You should expect to do no less than what He does. You abide in Him.

Well, if you say you abide in Him, then walk like Him, talk like Him, bind like Him, and loose like Him. Cast out devils like Him, heal like Him, deliver like Him, and preach like Him. Why? Because you are in Him.

> And that he died for all, that they which live should
> not henceforth live unto themselves, but unto him which
> died for them, and rose again (2 Cor. 5:15).

If you are living for yourself, then realize that Jesus died and rose again for you. After all Jesus did for you, don't live unto yourself. Cancel your plans, get connected with Him, and start living for Him.

AMBASSADORS FOR CHRIST

Wherefore henceforth know we no man after the flesh: yea, though we have known Christ after the flesh, yet now henceforth know we him no more. Therefore if any man be in Christ, he is a new creature: old things are passed away; behold, all things are become new. And all things are of God, who hath reconciled [totally changed] us to himself by Jesus Christ, and hath given to us the ministry of reconciliation. To wit, that God was in Christ, reconciling the world unto himself, not [holding their sins against] them; and hath committed unto us the word of reconciliation (2 Cor. 5:16-19).

Paul is saying to put this Word of reconciliation in your mouth. Why? Because you are *ambassadors* (or representatives) for Christ. (v. 20.)

I am an ambassador. I represent Christ. According to this Scripture, we should represent Him everywhere we go and in everything we do. We should represent Christ in our love walk. We should represent Him in our meekness.

Look at your life, and see if you are representing Christ. You are an ambassador. You're not just a person who lives somewhere. You represent Jesus: the Person and the power!

You are like government representatives in foreign lands. They represent the authority of America and its president in other countries.

God Almighty is sitting on the throne in heaven; you and I are down here on this planet. On this planet, we represent God and His kingdom. We are His ambassadors.

> God gave you His righteousness, His name, His Word, His anointing, and His Holy Spirit so you would not have to do anything alone.

Let's get out of religious traditions. Religion has blocked this truth because a lot of our representing began and ended at church. You can't represent Christ by just sitting there. You have to move out and do something.

Opportunities present themselves every day. When someone in your office says he doesn't feel good, stand up and represent. When someone is having trouble in marriage, stand up and represent. When a friend is in the hospital with cancer, stand up and represent. Ask them if you can pray for them. That is some of the best representing you can do.

There is plenty to be done, but many are afraid of what people will think about us if they see us praying for someone in the grocery store. We are afraid of what people will think if they see us on the side of the street ministering to someone.

That is why God gave you His righteousness, His name, His Word, His anointing, and His Holy Spirit: so you would not have to do anything alone.

Spend time abiding with him. "Let your light so shine before men, that they may see your good works, and glorify your Father which is in Heaven" (Matt. 5:16).

Remember you are an ambassador.

RESTING IN RIGHTEOUSNESS

CHAPTER SEVENTEEN

As we near the end of this teaching, think about this: The devil is not going to roll a red carpet out for you just because you are getting revelation on the righteousness of God. You must push yourself to the next level in order for this revelation to bear fruit.

Your life will not change just because you've read about righteousness. It is not going to change because you understand it. Your life will only change if you take the next step and do what is necessary to become proficient in the righteousness of God.

One of the things I have mentioned several times is the importance of not allowing your works to determine your righteousness. The righteousness of God is a position. It is not only about the rights you have; righteousness is also about a position you have.

How you position yourself in the righteousness of God will determine whether anything in God's kingdom works for you. Your position in righteousness determines whether your righteousness works. If you feel guilty, something is wrong. If you feel condemnation, something is wrong. If you feel inferior, something is wrong.

There is a stance that you have to take to ensure your rights. As the righteousness of God, you cannot let any roadblock from the flesh or the devil jeopardize your rights.

In addition, it is not enough to simply take a stance once and forget it. We have to make a conscious effort to *stay* in that position. Your internal attitude positions you for external results.

Think about it. Guilt happens from within. Condemnation happens from within. Inferiority happens from within. They are all part of our emotions, and that makes them a part of the soul.

When we get into the Word of God, it will save our souls. However, we must understand that in the area of our righteousness, there is a constant battle raging in our minds. Your righteousness is going to be settled or lost on the battleground of the mind. Your experience of the force of righteousness operating on your behalf is going to be determined on the battleground of your mind.

> Let us draw near with a true heart in full assurance of faith, having our hearts sprinkled from an evil conscience, and our bodies washed with pure water. Let us hold fast the profession of our faith without wavering; (for he is faithful that promised) (Heb. 10:22-23).

Thank God for what we understand about His righteousness, but I am interested in our knowing what has to be done in order to see results. Seeing results is what I care about now, because I believe that the Bible will do just what it says. I want you to see the human part in this spiritual law.

Let us all come forward and draw near with true (honest and sincere) hearts in unqualified assurance and absolute conviction engendered by faith (by that leaning of the entire human personality on God in absolute trust and confidence in His power, wisdom, and goodness), having our hearts sprinkled and purified from a guilty (evil) conscience and our bodies cleansed with pure water (Heb. 10.22 AMP).

Now, you can test yourself on this Scripture. Just look at your actions. You can say that you rely on and trust God, but in reality you may be reacting totally opposite.

Often, we don't give God enough time to work on our behalf before we begin trying a second alternative. We do not make up our minds to stay steady until He comes through. You have to believe that if the Father says He will do something, then He will. You must learn to trust Him despite the circumstance.

Most carnal Christians will call you foolish. But there is going to come a time in your life when you must qualify this Word for yourself. Either it works or it doesn't. Either you believe it or you don't. You have to decide that for yourself.

Often, we don't give God enough time to work on our behalf before we begin trying a second alternative.

There have been times in my life when I had to completely rely on God and the truth of His Word. I had to make a choice: *Do I trust my heavenly Father to look after me and take care of me or don't I?* I had to learn that my confidence level was never going to increase if I kept putting my trust in someone else to help me work things out.

You are never going to learn how to fully trust in and rely on God and the integrity of His Word until you have learned to fully trust Him. It is that simple.

You may have already gone through things you did not know how to handle. But somehow you made it through.

Now you look back and see what God has already done for you, and trust begins to build on the inside of you. You must make it happen for yourself. You have to know in whom you have your confidence. I trust God. I trust Him with my life.

I had this same conviction years ago when I was teaching on faith, and I tried to figure out why it is so hard for people to walk in faith. It's because they lack confidence—the substance of faith.

Let us draw near with a true heart in full assurance of faith, having our hearts sprinkled from an evil conscience, and our bodies washed with pure water. Let us hold fast the profession of our faith without wavering; (for he is faithful that promised) (Heb. 10:22-23).

The profession of your faith is your confession. Your confession, the Word of God, will help build your confidence.

Faith is a vital key to building confidence in the Word of God as well as confidence in God Himself.

It was my confession of the Word that healed me. It was my confession of the Word that brought me out of the grip of death after an automobile accident. It was my confession that built the 16 million-dollar building where we presently have our church services—debt free. It was not a miracle. It was my confidence in God Almighty, knowing that I believe what I say and that it will surely come to pass.

Even if I begin by saying my confession mechanically, something happens as I continue to say it. My confidence begins to develop because I will believe what comes out of my own mouth before I will believe what someone else says. If I say that God is able 100 times, I will believe it sooner than if I hear you saying the same thing.

> Cast not away therefore your confidence, which hath great recompence of reward (Heb. 10:35).

Don't throw away your confidence. Why? A compensation of reward comes if we refuse to throw away the confidence we have in the Word of God.

When someone says that he is the righteousness of God in Christ Jesus, the only thing that empowers that statement is the type of confidence he has in his righteousness. If he does not have any confidence in his righteousness, he is simply making

What you hear will not profit you unless you mix it with your faith and then apply the corresponding action.

noise, with no compensation. The writer of Hebrews says your confidence produces compensation.

When we become so confident in the righteousness of God that nothing can move us, we call it rest. When we are extremely confident in something, we do not even labor. There is no struggle in our minds to try to convince us that something will happen. We are confident, and that confidence leads to rest. *Confidence leads to rest.* There exists no more labor.

There is a point of entering God's rest, but what happens when you get there? Great things happen that many of us have never known because we have never come into that place of rest.

> Let us therefore fear, lest, a promise being left us of entering into his rest, any of you should seem to come short of it. For unto us was the gospel preached, as well as unto them: but the word preached did not profit them, not being mixed with faith in them that heard it (Heb. 4:1-2).

The Bible says the only thing that happens when you hear the Word is that "faith cometh." (Rom. 10:17.) However, what you hear will not profit you unless you mix it with your faith and then apply the corresponding action.

"For we which have believed do enter into rest..." (Heb. 4:3). When I first read that verse, I thought, *Now I must judge my level of belief by the level of my rest.* We are quick to say that we believe, yet we continue laboring like nobody's business. But if we truly believe, we are ready to rest from our labors.

> For we which have believed do enter into rest, as he said, As I have sworn in my wrath, if they shall enter into

my rest: although the works were finished from the foundation of the world (Heb. 4:3).

The work to achieve our righteousness is finished. Jesus sat down at the right hand of the Father. He's done His part. The writer of Hebrews says it is time for us to enter into the rest that comes when the work is finished.

> For he spake in a certain place of the seventh day on this wise, And God did rest the seventh day from all his works. And in this place again, If they shall enter into my rest. Seeing therefore it remaineth that some must enter therein, and they to whom it was first preached entered not in because of unbelief (Heb. 4:4-6).

Notice your belief is qualified or disqualified based on your rest. There were people who did not enter into the rest because of their unbelief. That means there is a connection between belief and entering into the rest of God.

Now I have something I can use to gauge my belief level—rest.

There is a connection between belief and entering into the rest of God.

If you find you have not entered into rest, put your mouth to work and start confessing and meditating on the Word. Spend some more time with God, until you get to the point where your confidence kicks in and you can enter into rest.

One Christmas many years ago, the Lord told me to divide my paycheck among every family member who walked through the door. Honestly, I did not have a lot of rest about that. All I saw were my bills and $35,000 of credit card debt, yet I knew I had heard from God.

The first thing I did was take my Bible, put it on the end of my bed, get down on my knees, and stay there. I read every Scripture I could find on giving and receiving. I spent time thinking about what each one meant, and I began feeling differently about it.

Then I began to put the Word in my mouth, saying it loud enough for my own ears to hear it. Before I knew it, I could enter into the rest of God's promise to meet my needs.

Again, he limiteth a certain day, saying in David, Today, after so long a time; as it is said, Today if ye will hear his voice, harden not your hearts. For if Jesus had given them rest, then would he not afterward have spoken of another day. There remaineth therefore a rest to the people of God.

Let us labour therefore to enter into that rest (Heb. 4:11).

Labor to enter into rest, into the confidence, belief, and trust in the power of God.

How do we labor to enter into rest? Through professing our faith, meditating on the Word, counting our blessings, and looking at the hope we have in Christ Jesus. That is the only labor that will effectively gain the rest of the Lord for us.

For the word of God is quick, and powerful, and sharper than any twoedged sword, piercing even to the dividing asunder of soul and spirit, and of the joints and marrow, and is a discerner of the thoughts and intents of the heart (Heb. 4:12).

For thus saith the Lord God, the Holy One of Israel; In returning and rest shall ye be saved; in quietness and in confidence shall be your strength: and ye would not (Is. 30:15).

There is a time to move and to pursue and to pray, but there is also a time to return and to rest. The Lord God of Israel said that in returning and rest shall you be saved. In rest shall you be delivered. In rest shall you be healed. In rest shall you be free of debt.

Isaiah is telling us we are doing all the right things and we have made all the right choices to labor to enter into rest. However, if we do not enter into the rest of God, which is where our strength comes from, we will never see God fulfill His promises to us.

Empowerment takes place when a man can enter into the confidence and rest God offers to each of us. There is strength in resting. No matter what's going on, you simply leave it up to Him. You have confidence in knowing that whatever He chooses to do or not do will be for your good. It is a settled issue. God is going to take care of you.

I never question Him. I don't care if I'm in the driest place in the world. If God says to do a miracle service, my confidence is in Him and He will absolutely show up to do

Everything God has given us to do is designed to lead us to His rest.

what He said. As a result of my confidence, an awesome power will be released and it can be the same in your daily life.

It doesn't matter when He is going to show up. It is our responsibility to rest and have confidence.

I once heard a man of God say, "If you're willing to stand forever, you won't be standing very long."

> Be still, and know that I am God: I will be exalted among the heathen, I will be exalted in the earth (Ps. 46:10).

When will God be exalted among the heathen? When will He be exalted in the earth? *When we are still.*

Everything God has given us to do is designed to lead us to His rest. The hope you have accumulated in the past because of all the things God has done is directing you to the rest. It is time for the Body of Christ, to learn how to rest and have confidence in God Almighty.

If you are having trouble entering into the rest of the Lord, begin to pray in the Spirit for a couple of hours. Soon, the problems will diminish.

FEARLESSLY BLESSED

CHAPTER EIGHTEEN

As I told you earlier, this study on righteousness was birthed out of the questions that arose from my messages on prosperity.

I began to ask people if they were debt-free as a result of the teaching. While many people *had* become debt-free, the percentages never seemed to change. When I asked the Lord about it, He directed me to teach on righteousness. I then understood that there was a connection between the two.

Therefore, it is only fitting that the last chapter should come full circle to show you something more in the area of prosperity.

In light of the scandals that have destroyed or damaged a handful of major ministries, many people believe that "all preachers want is your money."

> **Satan has three strategies he uses on the Body of Christ: First, accusation; second, temptation; finally, deception.**

If you have ever made this comment, take this test: Go to the grocery store, pick up a box of cereal, and take it to the checkout counter. When the cashier begins to scan the item, stop her and say, "I am offended that you want me to pay for this cereal, because the cereal companies just want me to have a wholesome breakfast." You will quickly discover that all the cereal companies want is your money. All the restaurants want is your money. All the gas stations want is your money. Their motive is gain.

THE DOUBLE STANDARD

When someone provides a service or a product and charges for it, the motive is gain. But when a ministry needs funds to preach the gospel, we think their ministry should function without financial support or at least without the financial support of Christians.

The belief that "All preachers want is your money" continues to surface because of mistrust, convenience, and greed.

Satan has three strategies he uses on the Body of Christ: First, accusation; second, temptation; finally, deception.

Those are the *only* three abilities the devil has to use against you.

DEMONIC STRATEGY

Satan attacks the Body of Christ through deception so we will never experience the prosperity God has set aside for us. His motive is to stop all efforts to fully evangelize the world. Romans 10:15

says, "How can they preach except they be sent?" When Paul asks that question, he is talking about those who don't have the opportunity to preach unless someone provides the finances for them to reach their destination.

At the root of that phrase, "All preachers want is your money," is a plan by Satan to destroy what God said in 2 Chronicles 20:20: "Believe in (and trust) the Lord your God, so shall ye be established..." We love that part. But then the second part of that verse says, "Believe (and trust) and remain steadfast to His prophets, and you shall prosper."

The devil will try to undermine our trust for the prophets: those of God who preach the gospel. Without your trust in them, Satan has a legal right to keep you from prosperity.

The majority of God's people have not prospered because they do not trust God's prophets; therefore, when they hear the message of financial prosperity from a prophet, they think, *I don't trust you. You probably have wrong motives. All preachers want is your money anyway.*

As long as you are ignorant about financial prosperity, you will carry an attitude of mistrust, which will prevent you from experiencing it.

It is estimated that one out of every six Scriptures in the Bible has to do with money, finances, or some type of material wealth. You would think as much as the Bible talks about finances, you would want to hear a message on financial prosperity at least one-sixth of the time.

But so many of us get upset and afraid that someone else is going to get a piece of us financially. Those feelings originate from a basic misunderstanding concerning biblical prosperity and the righteousness of God.

> It is estimated that one out of every six Scriptures in the Bible has to do with money, finances, or some type of material wealth.

In the Old Testament, no one ever dared to approach a prophet without a gift. (1 Sam. 9:6-10.) Even when Jesus came to the earth, the wise men brought wealth and riches to Him. These givers knew something.

Study the Bible. What you will find out chapter after chapter of the Old Testament is that every time Israel was in trouble, the people looked for a prophet of God that they could give to so they could be delivered.

Your prosperity is in the hands of your pastor, preacher, Bible teacher, evangelist, or whatever title they may have.

WHAT IS THE PROBLEM?

I find that some poor people are not concerned with the car their pastor drives. I also find that some rich people are not concerned either. Both wealth and poverty have a certain security about them, and neither of those groups seem to care what anyone else has or doesn't have.

But when it comes to the vast majority of those who are neither rich nor poor, there is an entirely different attitude. They seem to feel that since they work just as hard, they should have just as much as a wealthy person.

This is jealousy; a fear that someone is going to get more than others think they ought to have, based on what they are able to get themselves. Subconsciously, this behavior is like that of a child. They fear that someone is going to get a bigger piece of the pie. The underlying premise is that everything is supposed to be fair, and fair means equal.

Prosperity is a reward, not a wage. Hard work does not guarantee that you will walk in biblical prosperity. That walk requires understanding your righteousness.

Look at Psalm 112. In many Bibles, this chapter is titled "The Prosperity of the Righteous." In Christ you have a right, as the righteousness of God, to be extremely prosperous.

If you will walk in your righteousness, you will never be broke another day in your life. You will never be without the power of God or His blessing.

If you will walk in your righteousness, you will never be broke another day in your life.

Prosperity does not destroy you. Poverty does. Many people die because they are poor. They often cannot afford simple necessities, such as medicine, food, and rent. Poverty brings destruction. It is a curse, not a reward.

> Praise ye the Lord. Blessed is the man that feareth the Lord, that delighteth greatly in his commandments. His seed shall be mighty upon earth: the generation of the upright shall be blessed. Wealth and riches shall be in his

house: and his righteousness endureth forever. Unto the upright there ariseth light in the darkness: he is gracious, and full of compassion, and righteous.

A good man showeth favour, and lendeth: he will guide his affairs with discretion. Surely he shall not be moved for ever: the righteous shall be in everlasting remembrance. He shall not be afraid of evil tidings: his heart is fixed, trusting in the Lord. His heart is established, he shall not be afraid, until he see his desire upon his enemies. He hath dispersed, he hath given to the poor; his righteousness endureth for ever; his horn shall be exalted with honour. The wicked shall see it, and be grieved; he shall gnash with his teeth, and melt away: the desire of the wicked shall perish (Ps. 112).

Take a closer look at the word "blessed." "Blessed" means "empowered to prosper" or "empowered to have success."[1]

Who is empowered to have success? We are! Those who abide in God's righteousness shall be mighty on the earth. Verse 3 says, "Wealth and riches shall be in his house: and his righteousness endureth forever."

Notice the colon in that sentence. When a colon is included in a sentence, it means that the two parts of the sentence are connected to each other. The latter part is for further clarification or definition of the first part.

The King James Version has "shall be" in italics. Words in italics are put there at the privilege of the translator to clarify the passage. So remove the words "shall be." It says we *are* the righteousness of God, not "shall be."

Wealth and riches in his house now, not in the future.

"Well, Pastor, you haven't seen my house. There aren't any riches in that place."

It is important to realize that wealth and riches are there, although they are not visible to the naked eye. Remember the colon in the sentence. The clarification you need is in the second part of that verse: "and his righteousness endureth forever."

We could say it this way: "Because this man's righteousness is enduring, always present, and never compromising, wealth and riches are in his house." If you want the manifestation of wealth and riches in your house, then activate, practice, and develop your righteousness.

YOU HAVE RIGHTS

Wealth and riches are in the house of those who are the righteousness of God. He calls wealth and riches, or prosperity and welfare, as *The Amplified Bible* says, the *right* of those who are the righteousness of God.

Wealth is my right.

Prosperity is my right.

As incredible as it may seem, it is totally true.

I am the righteousness of God, and for me to let someone talk me out of my rights is for me to allow them to talk me *into* being a coward. I am not a coward. Wealth is my right. Riches are my right. Healing is my right. Answered prayer is my right—all according to the Word of God.

Some feel better if they focus on all those other spiritual things because then they don't see wealth and riches as their right. It is camouflaged, and they can ignore it because they do not exactly know what to do with it.

All along, the devil will attempt to talk you out of your rights. Have you been reluctant to prosper because you felt that as a Christian you should not prosper?

Well, if that is true, someone should have told Jesus to tell those wise men, "Take that gold and frankincense and myrrh back. I can't take it because I don't want to appear materialistic."

Unto the upright there ariseth light in the darkness...
(Ps. 112:4).

This refers to the revelatory gift of wisdom in your life. You have a right to wisdom.

...he is gracious, and full of compassion, and righteous. A good man showeth favour, and lendeth: he will
guide his affairs with discretion [or judgment]. Surely he
shall not be moved for ever: the righteous shall be in everlasting remembrance (Ps. 112:4-6).

What is he remembering? His righteousness. If you are constantly conscious of your righteousness, then you cannot be

moved by circumstances or pressure. You can stand on the Word of God fearlessly.

The rest of Psalm 112 contains more blessings and benefits only for the righteous, until verse 10. The psalmist shifts gears here, and if we are not careful, it can be missed.

> The wicked shall see it, and be grieved; he shall gnash with his teeth, and melt away: the desire of the wicked shall perish (Ps. 112:10).

What is the wicked man grieved about? Look at the preceding verse: "He hath dispersed, he hath given to the poor; his righteousness endureth for ever; his horn [his position and authority] shall be exalted with honour" (v. 9).

First, this righteous man dispersed and gave to the poor. He not only gave alms; he also helped to meet the needs of other believers. Now, it seems to me that you could not disperse if you did not have any money.

Second, as a result of his giving, this man's right standing endures forever. It becomes a shield around him.

Third, his position and authority will be lifted up in honor. The very thing the devil wants for himself belongs to the righteous man because of his generosity and compassion. The righteous man is not afraid to give, because he knows God, and not his job, is his source.

The righteous man is not afraid to give, because he knows God, and not his job, is his source.

The wicked suffer shame. God says He will bless the righteous in such a way that the wicked will see it. He is literally going to do it "in their faces." That is God's style. Remember, Jesus made an open show of the devil when He went to hell and led those in captivity free. (Col. 2:15.)

The wicked suffer grief. Grief is a sense of loss. The wicked grieve because they wonder how all that money was transferred to Christians. The Bible prophesies greater grief, because huge amounts of wealth are preparing to be transferred. (James 5:1-8.)

People do not become rich when everything is going well. Wealth is often transferred during bad times.

God will begin to reveal things to you because you are the righteousness of God. He will show you how to invest. He will show you how to sow. He will show you how to harvest.

The wicked suffer from anger:

> The wicked man will see it and be grieved and angered... (Ps. 112:10 AMP).

A man once told me that he did not like my lifestyle because I had too much abundance. He began questioning where the money he sent to my ministry was going.

He did not realize that I did not need his money. I'm the righteousness of God. I do not have to depend on my job, my ministry, or anything else. God alone is my Source. And as I sow, He gives. It's the principle of seed time and harvest.

> ...[The wicked] shall gnash with his teeth (Ps. 112:10).

That is the reaction of anger. The wicked will be so angry at the prosperity of the righteous that they will gnash their teeth at your prosperity.

The wicked suffer despair. They will plan and scheme. They will think they are going to get the upper hand and leave you sitting in the dust because they consider themselves to be wiser. They may be wise, but your righteous wisdom is better. Your wisdom concerning your righteousness in Christ will put their plans to shame. All their desires to harm, scam, embarrass, or do anything else to you, will come to nothing.

Not only that, but they despair over it.

> ...and disappear [in despair]; the desire of the wicked shall perish and come to nothing (Ps. 112:10 AMP).

People don't have a lot to look forward to when they go against the righteousness of God.

Wealth and riches are your right.

> But thou shalt remember the Lord thy God: for it is he that giveth thee power to get wealth, that he may establish his covenant which he sware unto thy fathers, as it is this day (Deut. 8:18).

It is God's desire that the wealth He puts in your hands be used to further the Gospel as He directs. If you are walking in your righteousness, then you will do that almost automatically.

I have recently conducted several conventions in foreign nations that rank among the poorest in the world, including Africa,

New Zealand, and areas in the Caribbean. I have conducted meetings in Papua, New Guinea, Australia, and London, where only three percent of church members tithe. Praise God, everywhere I have preached this message, the economy, at least among the believers, is changing.

Therefore, how can I preach unless I am sent? How can I share these world-changing truths if I cannot afford to get there? If I were struggling financially, could not afford to pay bills, and had to settle for less, then the cry across the world would not matter. I would not be able to help them. It takes money to get the ministry team and all the equipment over there: nearly $70,000 in fuel and preparations to travel and preach in those countries. It takes finances. You must be sent.

As a child, when my mother used to send me to the grocery store, she not only told me to go, she gave me money to buy what was needed. She equipped me with what was necessary to make the exchange.

The incredible part of all this is the fact that the reward for the one who goes and the reward for the one who provides the means to go is exactly the same. God values the demonstration of righteousness by rewarding the one who sends the prophet. The giver's reward is the same as the prophet's. (Matt. 10:41.)

YOUR JOURNEY IN THE RIGHTEOUSNESS OF GOD

I hope you now have a much better understanding of your position in the kingdom of God as the righteousness of God in Christ.

You have embarked on a journey and once you are finished reading this book, you will be held accountable for what you know.

My prayer for you throughout this entire book has been that your mental understanding would lead to faith and that your faith would continue to build your confidence.

It is also my prayer that your confidence would release your authority and that your authority would tap into God's power to give you rest.

Righteousness is the centerpiece on which Christian faith is built.

Remember, righteousness is the ability to stand before God without the sense of guilt, shame, or inferiority; just as if sin had never existed. It is the master key that unlocks the blessings that have been promised to us and paid for by the blood of Jesus. It is the centerpiece on which Christian faith is built.

As you begin to walk out this righteousness, you will learn not to expect anything other than God's absolute best in your life. You will begin to gain an understanding of God's plan for man in order to open up the treasures of the kingdom of God. God wants you to walk in His prosperity. He wants you to be completely whole in your body. He wants you to walk in all that you are called to do, in full confidence that you can do it.

It is up to you to conform continually to the image of righteousness by declaring who you are in Him. You are an heir of God. You are anointed. You are healed. You have the power to get wealth. Victory is yours. You rule and reign in life. There is a mark that has been made in your life that cannot be erased. You possess the master key that unlocks the fullness of what God has to offer. What is that master key? The righteousness of God!

AFTERWORD
A DECISION FOR ETERNITY

We have covered some life-changing principles in this book. But the only way to walk in these principles is to have a living relationship with Jesus Christ. If you have never declared Jesus Christ as the Lord and Savior of your life, here is your chance.

God loves you and sent Jesus to take your punishment for sin. If you will receive Him as Lord and Savior, all your sin will be forgiven instantly and you will become a new creation; your sin nature will die, and your spirit will come alive on the inside with the life of God and His righteousness.

I invite you to pray this prayer to God, from your heart.

God, I confess that I am a sinner. The sin nature has been alive in me, and I do not want it to rule me any longer. I repent of my sins, and I ask You to forgive me. I believe Jesus is Lord and that You raised Him from the dead. I receive Jesus, as my personal Lord and Savior. Come and live in me, abide in me. I receive the free gift of Your righteousness. Thank You for saving me and making me a joint heir with You!

Now, if you just prayed that prayer, you are a born-again Christian. Heaven is your eternal home, righteousness is your gift, the Holy Spirit is alive on the inside of you, and all your sins have been forgiven. Now you can walk in the righteousness of God.

Congratulations and welcome to the family of God!

Now I want you to do three things.

1. Write me at the ministry address in this book and tell me of your decision.

2. Find a Bible-believing church near you and start attending. It's necessary to partake of solid teaching, fellowship, and worship in order to grow as a believer.

3. Be baptized in water. Do that in obedience to Him, and follow it up by receiving the baptism of the Holy Spirit with the evidence of speaking in tongues. The Bible-believing church you become a part of can assist you.

For more information on any of this teaching, include that request when you write to me. God bless you!

ENDNOTES

Chapter 1

[1] Vines, s.v. "Justify," Vol. 1, p. 338-339.

Chapter 3

[1] Merriam-Webster's Collegiate Dictionary, 10th Ed., s.v. "vital."

Chapter 7

[1] The Chumash, commentary on Bereishis/Genesis 2:7, p. 11.

[2] Strong's, "Hebrew," entry #430.

Chapter 10

[1] Vines, s.v. "reconcile," p. 513.

[2] Vines, s.v. "atone," Vol. 1, p. 11.

[3] Strong's, "Greek," entry #2643.

[4] Vines, s.v. "life," Vol. 1, p. 367.

Chapter 14

[1] Strong's, "Hebrew," entry #7965.

Chapter 15

[1] Strong's, "Greek," entry #2137.

[2] Vines, s.v. "prosper," p. 495.

[3] Strong's, "Hebrew," entry #7919.

Chapter 16

[1] Strong's, "Greek," entry #2842.

[2] Vines, s.v. "Abide," Vol. 1, p. 1.

Chapter 17

[1] John 1:1-4,14 AMP

Chapter 18

[1] Vines, s.v. "blessed" Vol. 1, p. 19.

REFERENCES

King James Version/Amplified Bible Parallel Edition, Grand Rapids, Michigan, Zondervan Publishing House, 1995.

Merriam-Webster's Collegiate Dictionary, Tenth Edition. Springfield, MA: Merriam-Webster, Inc., 1994.

Scherman, Rabbi Nosson, *The Chumash,* Mesorah Publications, ltd., ArtScroll Series®, The Stone Edition, 1998, 2000, Brooklyn, NY, page 11—commentary on Bereishis/Genesis 2:7.

Strong, James, *The New Strong's Exhaustive Concordance of the Bible,* Thomas Nelson Publishers, 1995.

Vine, W.E., *Vines Complete Expository Dictionary of Old and New Testament Words,* Thomas Nelson, Inc., 1996.

ABOUT THE AUTHOR

An anointed teacher and conference speaker, Dr. Creflo A. Dollar Jr. is the pastor and founder of *World Changers Church International,* a non-denominational church located in College Park, Georgia.

Dr. Dollar received the vision for World Changers Ministries (WCM) in 1981, while a student at West Georgia College. God instructed him to teach the Body of Christ the Word of God with simplicity and understanding. In February 1986, World Changers Church International held its first worship service with only eight members at Kathleen Mitchell Elementary School in College Park. Attendance grew rapidly, and as a result, the ministry relocated to a modest-sized chapel, then later moved to its present location— the 8,500-seat World Dome.

A world-renowned author, Dr. Dollar has also written several books that cover a variety of topics, including debt-cancellation, healing, prosperity, prayer, family, and victorious living. Many of his past works, including *The Anointing to Live, Understanding God's Purpose for the Anointing* and *The Divine Order of Faith* have been added to the curriculum of several Christian colleges across the United States.

His latest releases include: *No More Debt! God's Strategy for Debt Cancellation* and *Lord, Teach Me How to Love.* In addition, Dr. Dollar is also the publisher of *Changing Your World* Magazine, an inspirational monthly publication.

Recognized for his cutting edge revelation and humorous, pragmatic approach, Dr. Dollar received his Doctor of Divinity Degree from Oral Roberts University in 1998 and serves on the Board of

Regents. His teachings have enabled thousands to experience financial breakthrough, restoration, and healing as a result of applying the simple biblical principles outlined in each teaching.

A successful businessman and entrepreneur, Dr. Dollar and his wife, Taffi, established the Word-based record company, Arrow Records, in 1998. An affiliate of World Changers Ministries, its goal is to promote gospel music that pierces the heart through a variety of musical styles. He is also the president and founder of International Covenant Ministries (ICM), an organization that provides an avenue whereby independent churches from around the world can come together and exchange ideas, experiences, and resources to promote unity and maximize vision.

Both Dr. Dollar and Taffi Dollar can be seen and heard worldwide through the *Changing Your World* Conventions and the *Changing Your World* radio and television broadcasts. With officess in Australia, the Republic of South Africa, and the United Kingdom, they are truly setting the standard for excellence in ministry and making a mark in the lives of millions that can never be erased!

To contact Dr. Creflo A. Dollar Jr., write:

Creflo Dollar Ministries
P.O. Box 490124
College Park, Georgia 30349

Please include your prayer requests
and comments when you write.

OTHER BOOKS BY
DR. CREFLO A. DOLLAR JR.

Available from your local bookstore.

If you have prayed the prayer to receive Jesus Christ as your Savior, or if this book has changed your life, we would like to hear from you. Write to:

Harrison House Publishers
P.O. Box 35035
Tulsa, Oklahoma 74153

You can also visit us on the web at
www.harrisonhouse.com

THE HARRISON HOUSE VISION

Proclaiming the truth and the power

Of the Gospel of Jesus Christ

With excellence;

Challenging Christians to

Live victoriously,

Grow spiritually,

Know God intimately.